Welcome to our SCRAPBOOK

STUDIO PRESS

Written by Julie Bower and Anthony MacMurray
Edited by Frankie Jones
Designed by Claire Munday

This edition published in 2018 by Studio Press
An imprint of Kings Road Publishing
Part of Bonnier Publishing
The Plaza, 535 King's Road,
London, SW10 0SZ

www.bonnierpublishing.co.uk

Paperback – 9781787412866

Ebook – 9781787414365

I cannot tell you what a thrill it is for me to introduce this book to you.

As you know, my friends and I have been through a lot together: falling out, making up again, fashion disasters, school clubs, homework nightmares... that time Jas sent Ollie and Rob to the moon in a pretend space rocket... crazy times!

But, through it all, we have tried to stay cool, sophisticated, dignified, even. And this is our chance to pass on our knowledge, so that future generations may benefit from our wisdom... well, I say 'wisdom'. To be honest, life is mostly just us messing up, getting it wrong and trying again! But then that's the same for everyone, right?

So, here it is! The *So Awkward Scrapbook*! It's mostly brilliant articles, newsletters and bits of writing by my friends and me, full of cool advice about how to live your life. (Oh, and some weird bits of emails and texts may have been slipped in as well by accident, but don't pay any attention to those!)

So, what have we really learned so far? It's easier to tell the truth than to cover up a mistake; you don't have to try so hard when a boy genuinely likes you; and never let Jas and your mum redesign your bedroom... oh, and no matter what, you'll be ok as long as you've got real friends.

Hope you enjoy it!

Lots of love
Lily
X

3

Hi Guys!

Lily asked us to write an introduction to the scrapbook, so here it is. She said we had to sound cool and sophisticated, and not go on about the time she tipped milkshake over her boyfriend. Or that other time she realised she was turning into her mum. Or that other time she threw tomato ketchup over herself. Don't worry, Lily! I'm not going to talk about any of that stuff!

I guess this book is a chance for me to share my advice with you all. As you know, I'm kind of the sensible one in the group. I've got an answer for every problem and people often come to me for my no-nonsense solutions. Although when I pointed this out to Lily and Martha, they fell about laughing. Weird, right?

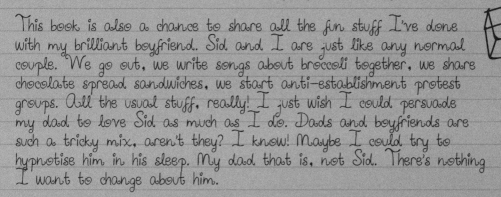

This book is also a chance to share all the fun stuff I've done with my brilliant boyfriend. Sid and I are just like any normal couple. We go out, we write songs about broccoli together, we share chocolate spread sandwiches, we start anti-establishment protest groups. All the usual stuff, really! I just wish I could persuade my dad to love Sid as much as I do. Dads and boyfriends are such a tricky mix, aren't they? I know! Maybe I could try to hypnotise him in his sleep. My dad that is, not Sid. There's nothing I want to change about him.

Sorry, what was I talking about? Oh yes! Anyway, welcome to the So Awkward Scrapbook! Hope you enjoy reading it as much as we enjoyed writing it. I have to go — I just dropped my chocolate spread sandwich and I promised Lily I wouldn't get any food stains on my introduction. It's fine — I don't think she'll notice.

Peace out
Jas
Xxx

 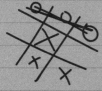 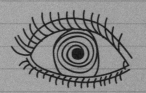 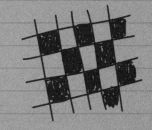

I'm going to keep this brief, as I am in the middle of some very important research. To be honest, I'm not sure why Lily is making us all write introductions to this scrapbook.

Surely it's perfectly obvious what it is - a collection of ramblings from the minds of a bunch of adolescents with limited insight into their failings. I'm far too busy making contributions to the field of science to bother with such nonsense.

I mean, obviously my article about kissing is incredibly useful. And mine and Ollie's newsletters are a fascinating read. Also, there's an amazing board game on page 96 and 97. I've already won five times...! Fine, I admit it, I've loved contributing to this book! Just don't tell Lily. She'll be all 'I told you so'.

Lily and Jas also think I should mention my boyfriend in my introduction. As I've told them a thousand times, Ollie isn't my boyfriend. Of course I'm more than happy to talk about his incredible brain, his admirable work ethic, the way his eyes sparkle when he's perfecting an equation... but to be clear, there's nothing romantic going on there!

That's all I have to say, really. In summary, this book was a lot more fun than I thought it would be, and when it comes to love and boyfriends, I know nothing and intend to keep it that way.

As Einstein once said: 'The important thing is not to stop questioning.' I guess asking the right questions is better than knowing all the answers. Which is just as well, really!

Kind regards,
Martha
x

$$a + b = 26$$
$$a - b = 18$$

$$3x + 5 - 5 = 20 - 5$$
$$3x = 15$$

CONTENTS

Lily 🖤

Martha
Fitzgerald

Jas

Ollie

Sid

Rob

LILY'S GUIDE TO...
MANAGING YOUR MUM

Much as I love my mum she can be a bit embarrassing sometimes. I know she means well, but on those days when she's picking me up from school with green hair or calling me Lily Silky Bum Bum in front of my friends, I just want the ground to swallow me whole!

One good thing about it, after years of dealing with Awkward Mum Stuff (Or AMS for short) I've become an expert at mum management.

Here are my top five tips for managing your mum:

1. Don't panic. Next time she launches into the story of how the dog ate your knickers when you were five, remember to breathe and focus. If you panic, you might try to stop her by blurting out, "Look, everyone! My hair is on fire". Trust me, that never helps.

2. Be honest but kind. Sitting Mum down and begging her never to speak again in front of your friends might hurt her feelings. Try saying something like, "Hey, Mum, your stories are so funny that you're making everyone jealous! Maybe you should be less funny today."

3. Remember she loves you.
Mums have a funny way of showing it sometimes, but even when she's performing the Rudey Nudey dance you used to do when you were six, it's coming from a good place.

4. Be prepared.
My mum and I now have a system. When she's about to say or do some AMS, I wave my left hand. If what she's saying is fine, I wave my right hand. When I'm literally about to die of shame because of what she's saying, I wave both hands, stand on one leg and make a chicken noise (admittedly, this makes me look even more daft, but at least it stops her talking!).

5. Talk to your friends.
Don't let the AMS embarrassment keep going round in your head. Share it! Half the time it's never as bad as you think. Jas and Martha don't even notice Mum's stories anymore. In fact, I think Jas quite likes them, but that's another story...

Hi Guys!

Jas here, your resident agony aunt and one-stop shop for all your problems. Whether you're feeling sad, cross or just need a chat, Aunty Jas is here to help with a friendly ear and a warm hug. Have a read of my latest batch of letters.

They've all been written anonymously.
Can you guess who they're from?

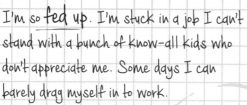

I'm so **fed up**. I'm stuck in a job I can't stand with a bunch of know-all kids who don't appreciate me. Some days I can barely drag myself in to work.
What should I do?

Yours depressedly,
I Hate Mornings

Dear I Hate Mornings,
Well, someone's wearing their grumpy pants today, aren't they? Look, I think I know who this is and take it from me, Sir, you're an awesome teacher! But if you're thinking about changing jobs, you just have to follow your heart. I know! You've always got jam on your tie, maybe you can be a sandwich maker...
Have fun!
Aunty Jas x

As you know, I don't like to complain. Anger is a waste of vital brain energy. However, I am disappointed to report that someone has recently borrowed my microscope and has not returned it. And yes, it has been three days now. Well, 3 days, 7 hours and 44 minutes. Not that I'm counting.
I guess some people don't respect important equipment. I guess some people don't care if they're standing in the way of progress. And, frankly, genius.
Yours frustratedly,
Science is King

Hi, Science Is King,
OK, OK, I get the hint! I'll give it back to you today. It's just a really good doughnut holder…
I'm kidding! I actually use it for hairbands :)
Jas x

Dear Aunty Jas,
OK, I'm writing this quickly because I need help and fast. My boyfriend and I always celebrate our first date anniversary (as well as first kiss, first time we met, first time he lent me a pencil, first time he said my name...), but I woke up this morning and realised I'd forgotten! I can't face him now. How do I tell him I forgot one of our anniversaries?!
Yours scaredly,
Worst GF Ever

Dear Aunty Jas,
Hi! Rob here! (Oops, sorry, was I not supposed to say that?) OK, this is weird. Lily's been avoiding me all day. I checked and I'm pretty sure it's not one of our ~~anniver~~ anniversaries. Has she said anything to you?

Dear Rob and Worst GF Ever,
Seriously, guys, talk to each other!!! It's like Sid always says, love is about talking, even if you've got a mouthful of cake. It doesn't matter if you forgot one of your eighteen thousand anniversaries! Celebrate the present, guys. Enjoy the now. OK, so now I've got myself thinking about cake. Time for a snack break!
Yours snackingly,
Aunty Jas

Dear Aunty Jas,
The unthinkable has happened! My arch nemesis and rival, Cassie, has beaten my top score in the school's chemistry quiz.
Obviously, I'm completely fine about it. Good for her, that's what I say! But, just supposing I wasn't fine about it... say I was seething with rage and desperate for revenge... how would that work?
Jas, I need revenge ideas.
Your evilly,
Chemistry Queen

BFFL

Dear Chemisty Queen,
I love coming up with revenge ideas! You could put jelly on her hairbrush. Or put a whoopee cushion under her chair on assembly day. :)
Although, thinking about it, is revenge what you really want? Maybe you're just cross with yourself for coming second. If you work hard, you'll be back in the top spot before you know it. And if you don't, maybe that's not so bad.
Sending hugs,
Aunty Jas x

THE WEEKLY CHECKMATE

Greetings and a warm welcome to all you fellow lovers of this majestic game! They say it's a sport of kings and we like to think we're bringing a slightly regal theme to this week's edition.

We're always looking out for new members, so if you're thinking of joining, don't be shy! But also do prepare to lose. We take it very seriously and we will show you no mercy on that board.
Can't wait to hear from you!

Lots of love,
Your Chess Club presidents
Martha and Ollie

CHESS PIECE OF THE WEEK!

This issue, the award for Chess Piece of the Week goes to... **the rook.**

Ah, the noble rook.

Sure, it can only move vertically or horizontally, but boy does it go as far as it wants up that board!

If I had a pound for every time this little baby got me out of a tight spot, I'd have £7.50.

FUN CHESS FACT OF THE WEEK!

Did you know, the first World Chess Championship took place in New York in 1886. The same year as the Treaty of Bucharest!

Cranmede School Chess Match Report
By Maxwell Tyler

An odd game this week. I was looking forward to being roundly defeated by my hero and mentor, Ollie Coulton.

But, weirdly, I kept winning! It was the easiest game I've ever played! I just kept beating him! Over and over and over again. By miles!

I'm sure he was letting me win, obviously. After all, he's older than me and he's been playing longer.

I mean, no way would he suffer such a humiliating defeat if he wasn't trying to let me win! I'm younger, I'm less experienced and, as I said earlier, I really did beat him by about a million miles.

I'd love to write more, but Ollie says there isn't enough room in the newsletter. Fingers crossed for next week!
Editor's Note: Thanks, Maxwell! Obviously, I was letting him win. Just clearing that up there! Ha ha. Maxwell. Such a kidder!

PLAYER OF THE WEEK
Profile on... Martha Fitzgerald

Favourite chess piece?
All of them are essential to the game. It would be counterproductive to pick a favourite because, as I say, you do need them all. Why would you even ask that?

What type of chess board do you prefer, wood or marble?
I don't really have an opinion. I actually think such things are a distraction from the game. It doesn't really matter.

Favourite move?
Again, it just depends. Sorry, who wrote these questions?

OK, moving on... favourite chess memory?
Well, no one forgets their first game. Do you remember, Ollie? You were crying because you'd just been beaten by a year 9 and...

OK that's all we've got time for this week! Thanks, Martha!

NAME THAT MATCH!

That's right! It's time for everyone's favourite weekly Chess Club newsletter challenge...
Name that Match!

Fans of the school chess team will remember my classic stonewall from last weekend's tournament *(see opposite)*.

But which match was it from?

a) The 10 a.m.
b) The 11 a.m.
c) The 12 p.m.

Email your answers to the usual address. Good luck, guys!

Lily's Guide to Getting Over Them

OK, so the worst has happened. You thought it was special, that your love would last forever, and now it's over. Gone. Finito. Or, as Martha likes to say, "Who? Sorry, why are we still talking about this?"

Whether it's your first break-up or your tenth, it's never fun when a relationship ends.

So you may have accepted it's over, but what now? How do you get through the next few weeks in one piece?

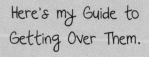

Here's my Guide to Getting Over Them.

Don't feel bad for feeling bad. It's OK to feel sad. Ditto angry, embarrassed, confused and anything else you happen to be feeling. It's normal and healthy to spend time sobbing into your ice-cream soaked pyjamas, so don't fight it. Take that time. Make the most of it. (Just remember to wash your pyjamas when the smell gets too much!)

Talk the talk. At first, it's like they're on your mind 24/7. The memories, the hurt… it's good, it's real and you need to get it out there. Share every feeling, every thought with anyone who you trust (just try to notice when their eyes glaze over). True friends will always let you bore them for a few weeks, but remember to return the favour when it's their turn.

Don't take it personally. When you really care about someone and things don't work out it can feel like the whole world is laughing at you. The truth is, break-ups are just an annoying part of life and it really does happen to everyone. Risking your heart is scary, but it's important. No matter how bad the pain or the embarrassment, it fades eventually.

Know when it's time to move on. One day, you suddenly don't feel like listening to that same song over and over just because it reminds you of them. And staring at their social media profiles for hours in the dark suddenly starts to feel a bit weird. The time has come to scrape the ice cream off your T-shirt, change the music and get back out in the sunshine again.

People often say to me, "So, Jas, which is your favourite pet?" And I'm like, "Don't make me choose!" The problem is, I love them all. Loggy the Log, Tamsin the Brick and especially Derek the Under the Bed Fluff. But I guess Hannibal the Rock will always have a special place in my heart, so I've decided to write about him.

CARING FOR YOUR PET ROCK by Jas

We all know everyone loves a pet rock. Why wouldn't you? They're cute, dependable bundles of love. However, a word of caution. Pet rocks need tons of love and affection and they can live for, well, forever really. They're rocks. So, before making the decision to get one, think carefully. Do your research. Ask yourself "What kind of rock should I get?", "Am I really up to the challenge of caring for these noble creatures?".

TYPES OF PET ROCK

GARDEN ROCKS are easy to come by but can be muddy, so you're going to need a scrubbing brush!

A piece of FLINT looks great on the shelf but takes a lot of polishing. Watch out for those sharp edges!

A PEBBLE makes a fun pet, plus they come in a range of sizes and colours. However, pebbles do get lonely, so you may want to think about getting more than one so they can keep each other company.

BOULDERS are not for the faint-hearted. They're also tricky to store and really heavy to get upstairs, so you'll need permission before bringing one home.

FEEDING

The good news is rocks don't need food. You may want to give it some mud from time to time as a treat, but as my friend Martha always says, "What are you doing? It has no mouth, no teeth and no digestive system! Get it away from me!" So this really is an area you don't need to worry about too much.

CAGE

Rocks don't really move much. They just sort of sit there, so you don't need a secure cage as they rarely try to escape. A good display case is ideal. Perhaps with some mood lighting so you can show your rock off to its full potential.

EXERCISE

Rocks don't really need much exercise (*see above*), but it doesn't hurt to get them out every so often for some fresh air and a little cuddle. I like to chat to my rocks because they don't judge and they don't answer back (I have a particularly friendly piece of granite at the moment which is a great listener!). Rocks also love hanging out with other rocks, so remember to socialise your rock any chance you get!

Hope this helps! If you follow my instructions above, you'll find you get years of happy rock-keeping.

Have fun!

Errrgh.

I agreed to help Rob with a report.

But I didn't know he meant a football match report!

I guess it's kind of Rob to share his hobby with me. But football and I are like two positively charged particles. We repel each other.

Anyway, since I couldn't get out of it, here it is:

Football Match Report:
Cranmede School Versus, um, the Other Team

By Ollie Coulton

2.45 p.m. I noticed the players lacing up their boots. From this, I deduced a game was about to start. I also deduced one team would be wearing blue, the other red. So far, so good.

2.50 p.m. Attempted football talk. Phrases like "I am excited about this football match. I wonder who will win," went down well. Comments like "Will this be over soon?" and "Does it matter who wins, you'll just do it all again next Saturday?" were less popular.

3 p.m. The game began, or 'kicked off', when a man in black, or 'Ref', blew a whistle.

3.05 p.m. The players ran around, presumably in pursuit of the ball.

3.07 p.m. They ran up one end of the pitch. Then they ran back the other way.

3.10 p.m. Then they ran up the other end of the pitch.

3.12 p.m. Then they ran back the other way.

3.32 p.m. Then... a miracle! Something happened! An alien spaceship landed and took everyone hostage! I'm kidding. It was just more running around.

3.40 p.m. Someone kicked the ball between the goalposts. Even with my limited understanding, I realised a goal had been scored. I leapt in the air, arms up. "Goal!" I shouted. "Goal! Hooray for the goal!"

3.41 p.m. I quickly sat down again. It was the opposition team who had scored.

3.45 p.m. Suddenly, things got interesting. I realised I could calculate the optimum angle a player would need to approach the goal in order to score.

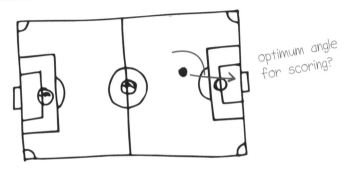

optimum angle for scoring?

4 – 4.15 p.m. More running around, shouting etc. Meanwhile I calculated the required velocity to run a football pitch in under 30 seconds.

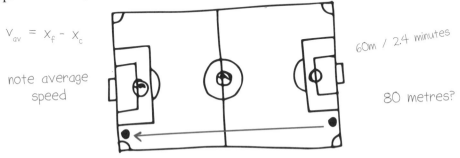

$$V_{av} = x_f - x_c$$

note average speed

60m / 2.4 minutes

80 metres?

4.30 p.m. Not sure. Maybe a goal or a penalty or something? I was too busy calculating the thrust-to-input ratio of the perfect shot.

4.45 p.m. Then, suddenly, it was over. One team won, the other lost, etc. And I had 20 diagrams relating to every aspect of the game!

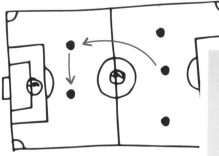

Although, I did wonder if it was maybe not exactly what Rob had asked for.

However, to my surprise, he thought my calculations were mega epic. Apparently, the coach can even use them for training AND he wants me at every match from now on!

Every. Single. Match.

I really didn't think this through.

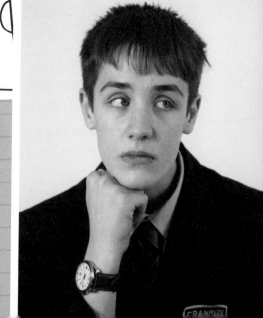

Hi guys! I'm really excited because I'm going to share the first two chapters of my very own novel! JK Rowling is one of my all-time heroes and she was a big inspiration behind me writing a book. And although this one hasn't got magic in it or anything, I plan for it to be a whole series of books, featuring the adventures of my heroine...

Can't wait to read!! Tas

Liv Hannington

The fearless globe-trotting TV reporter!

It's not too long is it? – Rob

Some people who've read these chapters (just my mum so far) have asked me where I get my ideas from and, well, I don't know, really. Just from the world around me, I guess. But I should say that any resemblance to real people is entirely coincidental.

It's been quite hard finding the time to write this, what with school, homework, after-school club, hanging out with Rob, doing chores and all the other millions of things going on in my life, so I don't know when it's likely to be finished, but see what you think so far!

HERO OF THE HOUR
A Liv Hannington Adventure

By LK Hampton

Chapter One

Famous and respected TV journalist Liv Hannington pulled up outside the headquarters of BNC News in her bright red sports car, a look of determination on her pretty but intelligent-looking face. Though only twenty-three years old, Liv had risen to the top of her profession with record speed and she was now the go-to investigative reporter whenever there was a national crisis or a cute animal in danger.

She got out of the car, grabbed her bag and brushed her shoulder-length brown hair out of her surprisingly soulful hazel eyes. After marching through the doors of the TV network building, she passed old Tom on reception and gave him a warm smile. *Some equations would go nicely here - Ollie*

"Morning, Liv," he said as he dragged a large sack out from behind the reception desk. "Got some more fan letters for you."

"Oh, thanks, Tom, I'll pick them up on my way out. I don't want to be late for this meeting."

"Right you are, miss," said Tom, appreciating the fact that Liv took the time to talk to him like an equal rather than ignoring him like some of the more arrogant TV journalists who worked at BNC news, who weren't even as famous or as good at their job as Liv was.

Liv got in the lift and pressed the button for the fifth floor, allowing herself a small moment to feel pleased about all the good work she'd done as an investigative journalist. There was the factory that she got to clean up its act, after she reported that it was polluting the environment.

I'm loving this already! — Jas

Liv Hannington really reminds me of someone! But who???

There's no such thing as llama-hunting - Martha

And there was the rare species of llama that she had helped rescue from extinction thanks to her undercover investigation into illegal llama-hunting. Being paid quite a lot, and being famous, and getting a big allowance to buy nice clothes, and getting her hair and make-up done professionally every day was all very well, but what really mattered, thought Liv, was doing something good for the world.

The lift pinged and Liv stepped out into the corridor, the look of determination she had earlier returning as she thought about the meeting she was about to have with her boss, Mr Jeff Lamone.

Mr Jeff Lamone? Don't let Sir read this!! - Sid

Jeff Lamone had become head of BNC news when his elderly father passed the company on to him the previous year. This had surprised and annoyed a lot of people, especially since Jeff had shown no signs of being good at running anything. He had been spoiled by his father and had spent his whole life sunbathing on a yacht in the Mediterranean Sea, eating ice creams and buying expensive guitars for himself, which he couldn't play, even though he thought he could.

Mr Lamone really reminds me of someone! But who???

Liv had always liked him, though she thought he was lazy. But his last email to her had made her very angry, indeed. Only those who knew Liv very well would have been able to detect this anger, however. One thing Liv prided herself on was always keeping a cool, calm appearance when she was angry, stressed or upset. Even when really annoying things happened, like her car tyre getting a puncture or a waiter bringing her cabbage when she'd already told them she didn't like cabbage. She'd just smile sweetly, shrug and say, "Oh dear", because she knew there was no point losing her temper over trivial things. Now Liv Hannington really doesn't remind me of someone!

Liv knocked on Mr Lamone's door, but there was no reply. Puzzled, Liv opened the door a little and saw Mr Lamone with his head on his desk, snoring loudly.

This wasn't the first time she'd found Mr Lamone asleep at work. He always had some excuse like he was 'just resting his eyes' or he was 'busy dreaming up new ideas to make the TV station more successful'. But Liv wasn't sure that any of these were true.

"Mr Lamone!" Liv said loudly, waking him up.

Lamone looked wildly around the room and gave a big sigh of relief when he saw it was Liv.

"Oh, thank goodness for that," he said. "I thought you were my dad for a minute. He said if he caught me asleep at work again, he'd seriously think about replacing me with my younger brother. Well, Liv, what can I do for you?"

I don't normally approve of fiction, but this is quite good.

Liv fixed him with a serious, steely glare. "It's about your email," she said calmly, but in a way that showed she meant business.

"Which email was that?" Mr Lamone said blankly.

"The one where you said that you're cutting my travel budget, so that in future I can only investigate things that are within five miles of my house!"

"Ah, yes, that one! Good idea of mine, eh? It'll save the TV channel thousands of pounds!"

"But," said Liv, trying to stay calm despite her anger and totally succeeding, "what about the fact that I won't be able to do my job reporting on all the bad things going on in the world, if I can only go as far as my local high street?"

"Ah," said Mr Lamone, leaning back in his chair in a very immature and careless way that Liv could see had the potential for him to hurt himself quite badly should he fall. "Well, don't worry about that," he continued. "I'm sure there's plenty of wrongdoing you can report on in the high street. Try the greengrocer's. I bet there's an apostrophe in the wrong place down there!"

Ooh, what a meanie!! — Jas

This last comment seemed to amuse Mr Lamone greatly and, worried that her famous powers of emotional control might temporarily desert her, Liv decided to leave and plot her next move.

As she walked down the corridor back towards the lift, she heard the satisfying sound of someone falling off their chair.

Turn to page 38 for Chapter Two!

BEST FRIENDS

ADVICE FOR TEENAGERS
BY MR MALONE

When I think about my teenage years, I wish I could have had a wise, mature (but young-looking), cool, funny and clever person around to give me advice. Well, you're in luck, Mr or Ms Teenager, for here I am!

DON'T WORRY ABOUT WHAT YOU LOOK LIKE

When you see me now – boyish good looks, strong sportsman's body – it's hard to imagine that as a teenager I really wasn't happy with the way I looked. I was worried about my lack of underarm hair, for one. But now, when I look at photos of myself as a teenager, I don't know what I was worried about! I was a perfectly normal lad. Who cares if I had smooth underarms? And anyway, I only had to wait another five or six years before hair grew there.

DON'T STRESS TOO MUCH ABOUT EXAMS

Boo! Exams! Who likes exams? I used to have this nightmare where I'd be in the exam hall and I'd turn over the exam paper and realise I hadn't revised. And in real life, too, I'd be in the exam hall, turn over the exam paper and realise I hadn't revised. Actually, maybe that's why I used to get so stressed...

REVISE FOR YOUR EXAMS

A good way to avoid getting stressed about your exams is to revise for them. And then do your best. That's all I ask of my students. No one really cares if you got an A or an A minus (unless you're Martha). And exams aren't everything. No one ever asks me what I got in my GCSEs (luckily for me, otherwise I wouldn't have got this job!).

FOLLOW YOUR DREAMS

If someone had told the teenage me that when I grew up I'd be a history teacher in a secondary school, I'd have screamed "No, no, no, no, nooooooo!!!" I'm not complaining about being a teacher. You get to go home at half three and have six weeks off in the summer – what's not to like? BUT! Part of me wonders whether or not the teaching world's gain was the music world's loss. I mean, anyone who's seen me performing my self-written songs knows that I'm a highly skilled singer-songwriter who could have been famous, just like... (kids, please insert name of current music artist here to make me sound like I've got my finger on the pulse). So I wish I hadn't been too shy to sing in public and followed my dream. Whatever your dream is, follow it!

DON'T BOTTLE THINGS UP

If you're worried about something, there's nothing worse than bottling up your feelings. When I was a teenager, I had a pet goldfish called Goldy. One day I found Goldy in his tank, lying on his side, completely still, floating on the surface of the water. I knew that this wasn't normal goldfish behaviour and had to accept that, sadly, he had died. I was so upset, but I refused to cry. Instead, I bottled up my emotions and tried to carry on as normal. A few days later, I asked Belinda Harris out on a date. She said no and I burst into tears in front of the whole class. Obviously, the bottled-up emotions I felt at the loss of Goldy had (like Goldy himself) floated to the surface. My classmates said that I'd cried because Belinda had cruelly rejected me. But they were wrong – I was far too cool to care about that.

Any more advice, you know where to find me! Try not to bother me before or after school, or during lunchtime or break, though.

Ollie

Are we still meeting at 9am as scheduled?

Martha
Of course. Library, usual table, advanced calculus, pgs 34 – 56 as per.

Excellent.

I mean you say of course. Only it's 9.03.

Martha
No. I make it 8.59.

It's 9.03. My watch has quartz crystal oscillators.

Martha
Mine is synched to Royal Observatory at Greenwich.

Yes but my watch is... Excellent! You've arrived.

Martha
You can stop texting me now.

Good point. FYI it is now 09.05.

Martha
Seriously?!

OK, I'm done.

Lily Hampton

Nickname: Lils, Lily Silky Bum Bum. (Thanks, Mum!)

Hobbies: Fashion, creative writing, hanging out with my friends.

Secret Crush: Dreamy naturalist Steve Bachelor... I mean my boyfriend, Rob obviously!

In ten years' time I will be... A famous novelist, intrepid news reporter or fashion journalist.

Most embarrassing moment: There was the time I pretended I was getting married, that time I lost it in front of the whole canteen because I couldn't do my hair, that time I got scared at my own Halloween party... and pretty much any time my mum did or said anything, ever!

Love is... My boyfriend's smile.

I couldn't live without... My friends.

Sid and I had an amazing time campaigning for the school council this year. We couldn't resist writing about it for the book! Here are some of our favourite campaign memories:

My Campaign Speech

Hi Guys! Amazing to see so many of you here! I know what you're all thinking. Why are Sid and J as campaigning for the school council? Basically, it started the other day when we were hanging out and talking about how much we hate injustice and war, and how there's never enough custard in the school canteen on Fridays.

And then Sid was like "Are you thinking what I'm thinking?" And I was like "Get to the front of the lunch queue quicker?" And then Sid was like "No! Let's run for the school council!" So please vote for us! Vote now, vote often. I mean you can only vote once, but you know what I mean. And, together, let's make this school a better, more custardy place for everyone!

1 Fairness for all

2 Justice for all

3 An end to war

4 Free the ants in the school ant farm

5 Free custard on Fridays

6 Free guitars for everyone

Sid's Campaign Song

The wind of change is blowin'
Blowin' through the hall
So let's all come together
And have justice for all.

We'll stand up and link our arms
And barricade the ~~front~~ door
Let's stand up and free the ants
And put an end to war.

Freedom's like a guitar
And guitars don't come free
But everyone will get one
If you just vote for me...

Would you vote for us? What would you like to see changed in your school?
WRITE YOUR CAMPAIGN PLEDGES HERE:

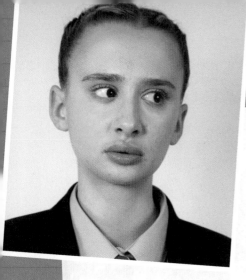

How to Make a Complex Gluten and Protein Mixture

by Martha

YOU WILL NEED:

Ground wheat powder
Unshelled chicken ovals
Sucrose
Lipid-based emulsion

METHOD:

1. Combine the lipid emulsion with the sucrose, ensuring hydration remains consistent.
2. Carefully add the wheat powder, allowing time for the proteins to bond and create gluten.
3. Add the sucrose and chicken ovals. Take care not to over mix to prevent the newly bonded gluten and protein networks from breaking down. Finally, place in oven to allow heat energy to transfer to the compound.
4. The protein network will harden, holding the carbon dioxide bubbles in place. The sucrose will prevent the starch molecules from crystalising too soon and the lipids will maintain moisture.
5. After 20-25 minutes, place your newly baked confection somewhere high up to stop Jas from eating it.
6. You can then share it with friends or as part of a celebration. Particularly enjoyable with a cup of infused crushed leaves in hot water.

*She means tea, guys!
Cake tastes good with tea, but
we already knew that, right?*

Chapter Two

Liv arrived at her smart three-bedroom house. It was a lovely property with a big garden and had been tastefully decorated by Liv herself, but it was by no means 'show-offy'. And considering how successful Liv was, it was actually quite humble and modest.

Liv came through the front door, dragging the heavy sack of fan mail behind her.

"Robin, I'm home!" she called.

Almost immediately, her incredibly attractive husband, Robin, came into the hall from the kitchen. They had been together for eight years since they met at school, yet the sight of Robin still made Liv's stomach do a funny flippy-over thing. It reminded Liv of their wedding day, only last year…

It had been an incredibly amazing day, like something out of a dream. And everything had happened exactly the way that Liv had imagined, making her months of meticulous planning all worthwhile. Liv had worn a beautiful and enormous white wedding dress, with cute little wild flowers in her expertly styled hair. And Robin had looked really handsome in a stylish grey suit that was both classically timeless and bang on trend. After the ceremony, which happened in a romantic old church, like something out of a film, 100 white doves had been released to form the letters L and R in the sky, just as they had been trained. All of Liv's friends and family had been there, and no one had embarrassed her by mentioning something silly she'd done in the past. Everyone agreed that she and Robin looked like the most amazing couple who had ever lived. Liv's mum, an expert cook, similar to Mary Berry, had made the most delicious and brilliantly decorated cake, which everyone had enjoyed and had even taken pieces home to eat later. Yes, it really had been the most perfect day ever…

I'm suddenly feeling quite sick, for some reason - Martha

Anyway, Robin came into the hall to greet Liv with a romantic kiss. He had a big smile on his face and Liv noticed that he had his hands behind his back.

"Oh, Robin, you haven't…?" she began.

"Yes, I'm afraid I have," said Robin as he revealed the gift-wrapped box tied with a big red bow from behind his back.

"Another surprise present? But that's the fourth one this week!" Liv exclaimed, shaking her head at Robin.

"I just couldn't help myself," Robin replied, shrugging his shoulders and smiling, making cute little dimples appear on his cheeks. "Aren't you going to open it?"

Liv sat down to open her present. Robin really shouldn't keep buying her presents, she thought, but that was just who he was, and there was nothing she could do to stop him being so spontaneous and generous and romantic. Plus, he was a successful premiership footballer and could well afford it.

"Oh, Robin, I LOVE it!" she said as she held up the diamond necklace, which was absolutely gorgeous but at the same time very tasteful and understated.

"I thought you'd like it," said Robin.

Liv had to agree that Robin always had a wonderful ability to choose gifts that she really loved.

"Why don't I make you a nice cup of hot chocolate, while you tell me about your day?" said Robin sweetly.

"But haven't you got football practice today?" asked Liv.

"I did, but I managed to get the day off so I could spend more time with you."

This Robin sounds a right drip! – Rob

Get the hint, Rob? – Jas   *What hint? – Rob*

Skip a few pages to find the rest of my amazing story.

39

Martha

Jas
Hey Martha! Guess who got a new phone contract with 100 free messages! I can message people all day, how cool is that?

Congratulations!

Jas
So… Whatcha dooooin?

I have that chemistry assignment. I thought we were covering covalent bonding formulas but I checked and it's supposed to be about exothermic reactions! I'm never going to get it done in time!!!

Jas
Cool.

Jas
OMG I think I just invented face toast!

I'm pretty sure that's already a thing. Stop texting me, I have to work.

Jas
You could turn your phone off?

Stop bothering me! Text someone else.

Jas
OK!

Lily
Martha, why did Jas just text me a picture of her toast?

LEAVE ME ALONE!

Lily
:0

Sorry Lily that message was for Jas.

Jas
Sorry Lily Martha is really moody today.

Err Jas? Was that message meant for Lily?

Jas
Ha ha! I hate it when that happens. Why do you keep texting me anyway, I thought you had an assignment?

I do Jas.

Jas
I wish you'd asked. I did exothermic reactions last week! I could've helped you.

Jas
Martha? Are you still there?

Why didn't you say something?

Jas
I didn't want to disturb you!

?*!*£$

Jas
I'll be right over. Love you buddy!

From: F Fitzgerald
Monday 13 September 10.07
Subject: Meeting

Dear Mr Malone,

I wish to discuss Martha's history syllabus. I am concerned that, as a gifted pupil, she's not being stretched enough to develop to her full potential. Please let me know the earliest time you can meet me.

Yours sincerely,
F. Fitzgerald (Mrs)

From: F Fitzgerald
Friday 18 September 11.14
Subject: Meeting

Dear Mr Malone,

Did you receive my last email about us meeting to discuss the history syllabus?

Perhaps you missed it or it went into your 'spam' folder.

Anyway, please kindly provide me with a date when we can meet.

Yours sincerely,
F. Fitzgerald (Mrs)

From: F Fitzgerald
Wednesday 23 September 09.03
Subject: Meeting

Mr Malone,

I am most concerned that you have not replied to my previous two emails.

If you like, I can email Mrs Griggs with my enquiry. I'm sure she would find the time to listen to my concerns about your teaching methods and your lack of response to parent emails.

Regards,
F. Fitzgerald (Mrs)

From: Jeff Malone
Wednesday 23 September 09.05
Subject: Re: Meeting

Mrs Fitzgerlad!

Sorry, just seen your email. You were right, went into spam. Why do they call it spam,
do you think? In my day 'spam' was meat you'd get in a can. Your mum would slice it up
and serve it with chips – delicious! Those were the days.

Anyway, thanks for getting in touch!

Cheers,

Jeff

From: F Fitzgerald
Wednesday 23 September 09.10
Subject: Re: Meeting

Mr Malone,

I suppose I should say 'thank you' for your reply. However, I'm not going to because it
was absolute drivel from start to finish. Rather than suggesting a date for our meeting,
you instead started reminiscing about the ghastly things you used to eat as a child.

Please reply with a date for our meeting.

F. Fitzgerald (Mrs)

P.S. In your last email you addressed me as 'Mrs Fitzgerlad'. This is not my name.
Please spellcheck your emails, as not doing so risks you looking like a complete fool.

From: Jeff Malone
Friday 25 September 12.55
Subject: Re: Meeting

Okay, bear with me Mrs F – Rome wasn't built in a day. And I should know, I'm a
history teacher!

Laters,

Jeff x

43

From: F Fitzgerald
Monday 28 September 9.03
Subject: Re: Meeting

Mr Malone, I do not regard 'laters' as an appropriate sign-off on a professional email. Nor the 'x', which Martha tells me means 'kiss'. Please do not write this in future or you will be hearing from my solicitor.

ONCE AGAIN, WHEN CAN YOU MEET ME TO DISCUSS MARTHA'S HISTORY SYLLABUS???

F. Fitzgerald (Mrs)

From: Jeff Malone
Thursday 1 October 12.55
Subject: Off sick

Thanks for your email.

I am currently not in school owing to illness. If you have an urgent enquiry please contact the school office between 8 a.m. and 4 p.m.

Regards,

Mr J. Malone BA (Hons)
History Dept.

From: F Fitzgerald
Thursday 1 October 14.37
Subject: Re: Off sick

Mr Malone.

You are not off sick. I have just driven past the school and can clearly see you in your classroom through the window.

From what I could see, you seemed desperate for the loo. But after speaking to Martha's friends on Skype, they think it's more likely you were playing something called an 'air guitar'.

I'm coming in to see you tomorrow at 4 p.m. sharp.

Sincerely,
F. Fitzgerald (Mrs)

From: Jeff Malone
Thursday 1 October 14.39
Subject: NOT TOMORROW!

You can't come in tomorrow, I've got a dentist appointment! I've got to keep the teeth in order. I mean, what would I be without my winning smile??

I have attached the full history syllabus for this year, so you can see all the things Martha will be learning.

Hope this will be okay for now, until I can find a good date for our meeting.

Soz!

Jeff.

jeremy_1.jpg

From: F Fitzgerald
Friday 2 October 09.42
Subject: CAT

Mr Malone,

The attachment you sent was NOT the year 10 history syllabus, it was a photograph of a cat.

Please send the syllabus immediately!
F. Fitzgerald (Mrs)

From: Jeff Malone
Friday 2 October 12.55
Subject: Re: CAT

Oh yeah, that was a picture of Jeremy, my new cat. Lovely, isn't he? My mum wanted to see him, so I took a picture.

I must have labelled the file wrong!

I think I've just sent the year 10 history syllabus to my mum!

What am I like??

Jeff

From: F Fitzgerald
Friday 2 October 14.37
Subject: Re: CAT

What are you like? I will tell you what you are like: you are a disgrace to the teaching profession!

I have REPEATEDLY tried to arrange a face-to-face meeting with you to discuss Martha's education and you have made NO attempt to make this happen.

This is your final chance, Malone.

WHEN. CAN. WE. HAVE. A. MEETING?

From: Jeff Malone
Monday 5 October 12.55
Subject: Computer Virus

Dear Parent/Carer,

Just to let you know that my computer recently got infected with a virus and I lost all my emails.

If there was anything you wanted to discuss with me, or if you would like to arrange a meeting, please get in touch.

Regards,

Mr J. Malone BA (Hons)
History Dept.

From: F Fitzgerald
Monday 5 October 12.56
Subject: Re: Computer Virus

AAAAAAARRRGGHHHHH!

Oh, dear. Poor Mother!

And you can really tell that deep down they really like each other – Jas

Can you?!? – Lily

Jas Salford

Best friends: Martha and Lily... and my dad, obviously.

Nickname: Ω, aka 'the symbol formally known as Jas' (I'm still waiting for that to catch on).

Hobbies: Potato sculpture, ant racing, dressmaking, darts, paper mache, curling, the kazoo, woodcarving, bell-ringing, taxidermy, yoga, baking, hopping, ventriloquism, escapology – oh! and I'm really into yoghurt. And crisps.

In ten years' time I will be... Touring the globe with my one-woman show: Stephen Hawking's *A Brief History of Time*, as told through interpretive dance.

Love is... The way I always get an itchy left elbow when I hear Sid's name.

If I had a million pounds I would... Finally launch my own brand of 'Crisp Yoghurt'.

Use this page to write down any thoughts you have. You never know when they might come in useful, perhaps for the novel you're working on or for cute things you want to say to your boyfriend.

Ideas for Novels

Idea for sequel to Liv Hannington: Liv moves to America and becomes a Broadway star?

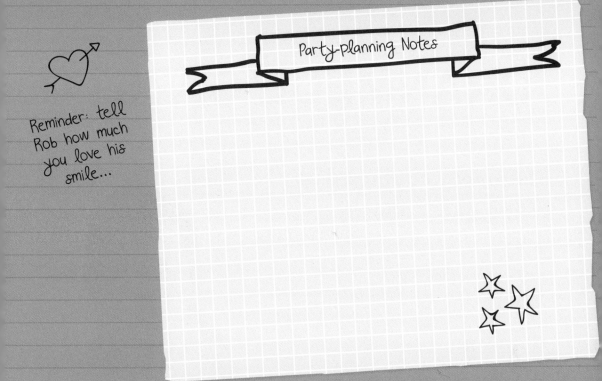

Reminder: tell
Rob how much
you love his
smile...

Party-planning Notes

Dates to Remember

REMEMBER: When you're
a parent you will never
embarrass your daughter.

CRANMEDE GAZETTE

YOUR SCHOOL NEWS DELIVERED DIGITALLY   PUBLISHED MARCH 2018

Stationery cupboard in graph paper shock!

Cranmede School is reeling today following the news that the stationery cupboard has once again run out of green graph paper.

"It's a catastrophe," said Martha Fitzgerald, victim. "It was there yesterday. I was hoping to complete a population pyramid today, but I guess that's out of the window. There's a rumour of green graph paper in the science block, so we're heading over there now, but who knows what we'll find."

Head of Year, Mr Malone said, "What? I don't know, use the blue stuff instead. Why are you writing all this down? Stop it! Leave me alone!"

Mr Malone being questioned on his knowledge of the graph paper situation.

HAVE YOUR SAY BY LILY

Last week we asked:
Do the boys' loos need repainting?

You said:

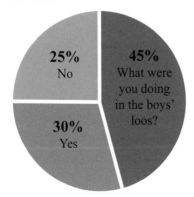

25% No

45% What were you doing in the boys' loos?

30% Yes

Thanks to all of you who replied!

Dates for your diaries:

Monday
Chess Club

Tuesday
Some sort of sporting event
(ask Rob Edwards)

Wednesday
Deadline for applications to
'Mathematician of the Year'

Thursday
Insect Club's monthly worm race; bring
your own worm

Friday
Sid's band to perform their latest song
'Float My Lemon', in assembly

A Day in the Life of Lunch

Intrepid reporter, Jas Salford, goes undercover in the school canteen.

They said there's no such thing as a free lunch, but there totally is!

When you're reporting undercover as a dinner lady, there's loads of stuff you can eat: cake, yoghurt, fruit – it's all just lying around! The tricky bit is blending in. I tried just putting one of those hair nets over my face, but that didn't work. And FYI, just putting a tea towel over your head doesn't

work, either… the best thing to do is hide under the table. And don't grab anything that's just come out of the oven.

Join me tomorrow when I'll be going undercover in… the school vending machine!

Exclusive! The answers to year 7's maths homework revealed by Cassie Coulton!

1. 76
2. 2 apples
3. 6
4. 23.8
5. A cuboid
6. 8.13 p.m.
7. 10 degrees
8. 4
9. 18%
10. X = 9

MALONE ALONE

Now on sale!

Ollie's binary word search

```
1 0 1 0 1 0 0 1 1
0 1 1 0 1 1 0 0
0 0 0 1 1 1
0 1 1 0 1
0 1 1 0 1 1 1 1
```

1	0	1	1	0	1	0	0	0	1	1	0	1	1
0	1	1	0	0	0	1	1	1	0	1	1	0	1
1	0	1	0	1	1	0	0	1	1	0	1	1	0
0	1	0	0	1	0	1	1	0	1	1	0	0	1
1	0	1	0	1	0	0	0	1	1	0	1	1	0
0	1	1	0	0	1	1	1	0	1	0	1	0	1
1	1	0	1	1	0	1	1	0	0	0	1	1	0
0	0	1	0	1	0	0	0	1	0	1	1	0	1
1	0	0	1	1	0	1	1	0	1	1	0	1	0
0	1	1	0	1	1	0	1	0	1	1	1	0	1
1	1	1	1	0	1	0	1	0	1	0	0	1	1
1	0	1	0	1	0	1	1	0	0	1	1	1	0
1	1	1	1	0	1	1	0	1	1	1	0	1	1

Jas asked if I would write this guide for ~~people~~ teenagers about heartbreak. I don't know why she asked me. It might have something to do with the fact she saw me crying in the library, but I was just having trouble with my contact lens. Anyway, having spoken to some of my friends, here's my guide on how to deal with having your heart broken.

<u>Dealing with Heartbreak</u>
By Rufus

UNREQUITED LOVE

A friend of mine had this crush on a girl. A beautiful, very intelligent, lovely, perfect girl. But when my friend asked her out, she didn't want to go out with him. Apparently, she was already going out with the coolest guy in school. This really, really hurt my friend, by all accounts. But the good news is he met another girl who liked him back. So my friend's history teacher was right when he said "There's plenty more fish in the sea, some of whom may fancy you."

BEING DUMPED

Another, different friend of mine was going out with a very kind and wonderful Spanish girl. They would spend every afternoon dancing the tango and speaking in Spanish. But after a couple of weeks she told him that she had fallen for the captain of the hockey team and this really, really upset this other, different friend of mine. But after she dumped him, he realised that he wasn't that into her anyway, so, y'know, meh.

FINDING LOVE AGAIN

The most important thing is believing in yourself. Just remember that everyone goes through heartbreak before they find 'the one'. As my history teacher says "Heartbreak is just all part of life's rich tapestry, Rufus."

Hope that helps!

My Love is Like the Deep Blue Sea

By Sid

(translated into whale)

Whaaoo**o**ogh
Whaooogh Ooooogh
Woooogh
Whaoooogh
Wogh.

Sid
By Jas
(Best accompanied on the bongo drum)

Sid,
I love the way you did
Share your yoghurt with me that time Sid.
Do you remember when you hid? During that game of sardines.
Sid, I wish we could get rid of war. But then what would we talk about?
We would have to talk about other stuff like Cupid. Or how to draw a pyramid, Sid

The Day We Met
By Jas and Sid

I still remember the ~~first~~ day we met
You were sitting on a chair or was it a net?
Your hair was up or it might have been down
You were wearing red or yellow or brown
But I remember your ears
Wooooah! I remember your ears
The first thing I said was is this seat free
And you were like yes or no or maybe
Or you might have just smiled or maybe you sn~~ee~~eezed
But one thing I remember and that is your knees
Woaaah! I remember your knees

I told you I liked you that very day
Or said something else in a roundabout way
We went for a drink or a walk or a ~~fast~~ snack
But one thing I remember and that is your hat.
Woaaah! I remember your hat.

Were you wearing a hat?

Someone was.

So true. Somewhere in the world, someone's always wearing a hat.

Rob's Good Boyfriend Guide

Um, OK, so Lily asked me to write something for this. I've given it a lot of thought and here's my good boyfriend guide...

1. Turn up
2. Say nice stuff
3. Try not to lose all the teddies

Lily here - I'm sure Rob MEANT to write A LOT MORE for this. He probably had to go to football practice or something. Anyway, I think he left out a few things that a good boyfriend should do, so allow me to add a few more ideas...

4. Make time for her. Yes, it's fun hanging out with your mates, burping or whatever it is you do, but your girlfriend needs to know she's important to you by making a plan to see her and STICKING TO IT!

5. Presents. You know how your girlfriend buys you little presents? Mainly featuring the letter R? They don't have to cost much, but they show you're thinking of her. And also that you're picking up on those little cute sparkly socks hints.

6. LISTEN! You know when your girlfriend has been sharing a heartfelt dilemma with you and finishes by saying, "What do you think?" and you go "Sorry, what? I was just composing my ideal all-time England football team?" That's REALLY annoying. Why not avoid the inevitable argument/sulking that follows by just listening the first time?

7. Smile. That's it, just do that smile you do. It's cute, okay?

We (that's Ollie, Jas, Sid and Rob) have been asked by Lily to come up with a career advice quiz to help you decide what you'd like to do after university, college or school

Take the quiz now and find out what job you should do!

CAREERS QUIZ

1. What's your favourite school subject?

a. Science
b. Art
c. History
d. PE

2. What do you like to do for fun?

a. Memorise the periodic table, do quadratic equations, look for new planets with your telescope
b. Invent dances, create works of art, make up songs
c. Stop wars, protest against inequality, fight poverty and injustice
d. Play football

3. What do you most often daydream about?

a. Winning the Nobel Prize for a world-changing scientific breakthrough
b. Sandwiches
c. The day all wars end and we all live in perfect harmony
d. Scoring the winning goal in the World Cup

4. Your friends would describe you as:

a. A genius
b. Hilarious
c. Having strong ideals and beliefs
d. Football mad

5. If you could travel in time, where would you go?

a. Paris, 1896, to meet Marie and Pierre Curie
b. A million years in the future!
c. Nowhere – it's all about now, man!
d. 30th July 1966, Wembley, to see England win the World Cup

6. Your ideal day would consist of:

a. School, chess club, TV's *Pointless*, homework, a TV science documentary, mapping stars, bed
b. Breakfast (full English, croissants, cereal), walk neighbour's dog, lunch at Big Sam's Sandwich Bar, invent invention, dinner at Pizza Perfecto, bed
c. Lie-in, breakfast in bed, write song, write letter to Prime Minister demanding a fairer society, get up, go on a march for peace, dinner, watch classic music videos on internet, bed
d. Watch *Football Focus*, play football, watch *Match of the Day*, bed

7. If you had a fault it would be:

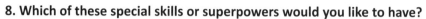

a. Don't get jokes
b. A bit clumsy
c. Too serious
d. Smelly socks

8. Which of these special skills or superpowers would you like to have?

a. Photographic memory
b. Ability to talk to animals
c. Play any instrument
d. Superfast runner

9. Which of these sets of guests would you like at your dinner party?

a. Albert Einstein, Richard Osman from TV's *Pointless*, Marie Curie, Martha Fitzgerald
b. Nikita Stricken (TV's Bug Lady), Keith Salford, Sid, an alien
c. Martin Luther King, Ghandi, John Lennon, Jas Salford, Nelson Mandela
d. Cristiano Ronaldo, Lionel Messi, Harry Kane, Lily Hampton

10. What's your worst fear?

a. Not getting a first-class degree
b. Never owning a dog
c. Losing the ability to play the guitar
d. Missing a penalty

Answers

Mostly A – you should enter the field of science and become a chemist, physicist, biologist, mathematician or astronaut.

Mostly B – you are super creative and should become an artist, designer, painter, author, poet, actor, singer or dancer.

Mostly C – you are politically minded and should become an activist, politician, revolutionary or radical thinker.

Mostly D – you are sporty and should be a sportsperson, athlete, sports commentator or PE teacher.

Mixture of A, B, C and D – you're complicated! Follow your heart! (Or ask your careers advisor.)

Ollie

It's here!

Martha
I can't believe it. After all this time!

Martha
OK. Send me the photo

Are you ready to see it?

Martha
Yes! I mean no, I mean will anyone ever be ready?

I know. Just breathe deeply. OK?

Martha
OK.

Martha? Are you there?

Martha
Oh, it's just got everything. Look at that radians function. Can I borrow it?

NO TOUCHING THE CALCULATOR. NO ONE MAY TOUCH IT!

Martha
Ollie we talked about this. You've gone over to the bad place again.

Sorry. I'll bring it over. Just wash your hands first, yeah?

Ollie Coulton

Favourite sport: Ha ha! Very funny! Good one.

Favourite colour: I hope one day to discover my own original colour. I shall call it 'Ralph'.

Favourite TV show: *Understanding Chemical Elements*, series 1-3 (series 4 was a let-down).

Favourite punctuation mark: Hmm, tricky one. I can never decide between the semicolon and the ampersand.

Favourite quote: 'A coefficient of friction is a value that shows the relationship between the force of friction between two objects and the normal reaction between the objects that are involved.' – Ollie Coulton (I know, I'm so sentimental!).

In ten years' time I will be... Still laughing at the 'favourite sport' question.

"Oh, Robin, that's so sweet," said Liv adoringly. Robin was always doing things like this. Even though he was a highly skilled and admired footballer with loads of fans, he always put Liv first.

"I could actually do with your advice," continued Liv.

"It's not about that silly Mr Lamone, is it? I've always said that you should be running that TV station, not him."

"Yes, that's what a lot of people say," said Liv. "But I prefer to be on the front line of investigations rather than just sitting in an office. Which is why I'm so annoyed that he's cut my travel budget!"

"What? No!" said Robin, shocked because he knew how much Liv cared about her work exposing all the bad things going on in the world.

Liv was about to go on, when there was a ring at the doorbell.

"I'll get it," said Robin helpfully.

And in a few moments, Liv's friends Marsha, Oliver, Jess and Stig were all sitting round the table with Liv and Robin, listening as Liv outlined her problem with Mr Lamone at the TV station.

"If anyone can help me," said Liv after she had filled them in, "it's you guys."

And it was hard for any of them to disagree with Liv, seeing as her friends were probably the cleverest people in the country and almost as successful as her. Marsha was Head Lecturer of Chemistry at Oxford University and her good friend Oliver had the same job at Cambridge University. Stig was a famous rock musician and political activist who had recently persuaded the government to lower the age of voting to seven years old, to give the younger generation a much-needed voice in running the country. And Jess was a successful inventor and TV presenter, who had her own show called *Sounds Like a Plan*, where people could send her a problem they had and she would come up with a plan to solve it, which always worked every time.

Hmm, Marsha, Oliver, Jess and Stig remind me of people... but WHO???

"Well, friends," said Liv, "what are your ideas?"

To be continued…!

Will Liv solve her problem with Mr Lamone while continuing to do her good work investigating bad behaviour and rescuing animals all over the world?

Will Robin score a goal for England and become even more loved? And will he keep buying Liv great presents?

Will Oliver finally reveal his feelings for his 'friend' Marsha?

How will Liv's plans for her and Robin to renew their wedding vows on a super-romantic holiday go?

Find out in the next exciting chapters of *Hero of the Hour* – a Liv Hannington Adventure.

Lily Silky Bum Bum! This is wonderful! Perhaps you could have a chapter where Liv spends a whole day with her amazing mum, where they go shopping, bake a cake and sing cowboy karaoke?

Amazing, Lily Love it!!! – Jas

Can I go and play football now? – Rob

A slightly far-fetched series of events, but overall a good light read. I particularly enjoyed the punctuation. 8/10 - Martha

A – A good essay on the identity of Jack the Ripper. Personally, I'm suspicious of this Mr Lamone character.

Er, Sir, did you actually read this?

HOW THE GANG GOT TOGETHER
A TRUE STORY, BY JAS

Lily asked me to write about how we all met. She also made me promise to tell the truth and not just make it up, so that's what I've done.

Here's my totally true, not at all made up story of how we all got together:

It was my first day at Cranmede School. I put on my jet-powered rocket pack and took to the sky!

The minute I hovered down in front of Lily I could tell she was impressed. She was all "Oh, Jas, you have to help me! I'm such a mess and need your awesome fashion advice!"

And I was all "Hey you look great as you are, you don't need to copy me." And she was all "No, I really do. If it wasn't for you I'd be crying in the loos!"

Then we found Martha crying in the loos. She had this really easy book of maths and she couldn't do it. Obviously I could because it was easy, but Martha wouldn't even let me help her.

I knew straight away that what she really needed was a boyfriend. I suddenly remembered this boy Ollie Coulton, who I'd also helped out that day. I could tell they were made for each other, so we headed over to the science block to meet him.

But then – disaster! An escaped lion broke into the school! Lily and Martha were too scared, but luckily I speak fluent 'lion', so me and the lion just ended up making friends. Anyway, we all found Ollie just in the nick of time and Martha and he were like "Wow, Jas, you're so right, we really fancy each other," and I've been the school hero ever since.

So that's how we all met!

The End!

Jas! This is libel! I did not fancy
Ollie when we first met! - Martha

Anyway, Jas, you were the one crying
in the toilets. You couldn't work the
vending machine, remember? - Lily

Well, I may have misremembered
a few things. One thing is true, though
- we've all been friends ever since.
Or: "Raaagh raaagh" as the lions say
- Jas

It's important to show your workings, so I've reserved a page in this 'scrapbook' for any equations, sums or experiments you need to write out in full.

Solve these equations:

What is the value of v if u = 10, a = 3 and t = 2 in the formula u = v + at?

How can you make x the subject of the formula 3x + 2y = 7?

What is the value of z if y = 2 in the formula 2z + 5y = 9?

10c − 8 = 12

Aim

Prediction

Explain
why you
think this
will happen

Apparatus

Method

Data

Results

Conclusion

11c + 11 = 33

67

From: charles.kane@cranmedechronicle.co.uk
To: jeff.malone@cranmedeschool.ac.uk

Subject: Re: Lily Hampton Work Experience

Dear Mr Malone,

As requested, I am writing to tell you how Lily got on with her work experience at *The Chronicle*.

First, let me say it was a pleasure to welcome Lily into our offices. She is a credit to your school – charming, intelligent and very enthusiastic. So enthusiastic that when I asked her to make the tea, she came back not only with the tea, but also with a 500-word exposé about the poor hygiene standards in the kitchen.

I wasn't intending for her to write stories for the paper, but after she asked me approximately 30 times a day, I sent her and an experienced journalist to cover the re-election of the leader of the council. I later learned that the leader of the council had resigned after Lily had subjected her to a series of difficult questions about the borough's poor provision of cycle lanes and failure to meet recycling targets.

Lily's next assignment was covering a football match between Cranmede School and King's Park Grammar. For this report, rather than writing about the match as a whole, she instead wrote a highly favourable minute-by-minute description of the actions of a single player, one Rob Edwards. A very interesting approach!

I would say that Lily can have a full-time job as a reporter here any time, but I think we're too small for her. I fully expect her to be editing a national newspaper in five years' time.

Sincerely,

Charles F Kane
Editor-in-Chief

https://www.myface.me.uk/RobEdwards

Rob Edwards

Nickname: Rob.

Full name: Rob Shirley Edwards.

Hobbies: Football, hanging out with friends, trying to
                                     figure out what Ollie is talking about.

Favourite possession: My lucky football socks.

Favourite smell: The smell of my lucky football socks... I
                                     mean my girlfriend's hair.

Favourite subject: PE, history. I'm Mr Malone's star pupil (he
                                     just keeps pretending I get the answers
                                     wrong so the others don't feel bad).

**If I had a million   Well, footballs are £29.99, so I would buy,
pounds I would buy:**   erm... 795,605 of them.

**In ten years' time I will   Really old! I just hope I still have all my hair.
be...**

Hi cats! Sid here with a round-up of what's floating my lemon sound-wise this week.

I believe music is, like, the soundtrack to our lives. Wow, that's kinda poetic. Must use that in a song. Anyway, I never go anywhere without being able to wire up some solid tunes slap bang into my lugholes. So, what am I digging right now?

HEAVY WHITE GOODS

First up, a bunch of groovesters who are never off my playlist these days. They're called Heavy White Goods and they're four teenagers from Norway whose instruments are kitchen appliances. There's Leif Hanson on fridge, Kris Olsen on washing machine, Ken Larson on microwave and Lars Johansson on dishwasher. These guys know how to rock! When Kris puts his washing machine on spin cycle and Lars gets his microwave pinging, you just have to get up and dance!

HEAVY WHITE GOODS

Lyrics 4
Danceability 10
Vibes 7

Overall 9

BOB ZERO

I'm also loving the fantastic minimalist style of Bob Zero. Bob arrived on the scene with an album of brilliant instrumental tracks called *Music*. There was no singing on there, just fantastic tunes. He followed this up by going completely the other way and doing an a capella album called *Voice* – no music this time, just him singing his songs, without any musical accompaniment. But in his latest album, he gives us the best of both worlds and has no singing OR music. Called *Nothing*, it's my fave chill-out album and listening to it is a great way to relax.

BOB ZERO NOTHING

Lyrics 6
Danceability 3
Vibes 10

Overall 7

JEFF MALONE

MALONE ALONE

I have to give a mention to the album *Malone Alone* – a set of acoustic guitar numbers from singer-songwriter Jeff Malone (also known as Mr Malone, my form tutor). I've been listening to this one quite a lot – mainly because Mr Malone said he'd test me on it later. What can I say about this one that won't get me into trouble? Well, I can deffo say it's like nothing I've ever heard before. Mr Malone has a really original way of playing the guitar, and the sounds that come out of it are way surprising and unusual. The songs are really 'from the heart'. You can really hear his pain in track four, 'I Hate Marking', there's a sad feel to the gentle ballad '(Please) Take Me Seriously' and a lot of anger coming through on the last track, simply called 'Mrs Griggs'. If you get your kicks from far-out stuff, this'll mash your spuds good!

Lyrics 4

Danceability 8

Vibes 6

Overall 7

NEXT DOOR'S CAT

Right now, I'm also enjoying Next Door's Cat. I don't know if it's angry because another cat's invading its territory or it's just hungry, but every night at about ten o'clock it makes some of the most interesting noises I've heard this year! I always find myself singing along, until my neighbour rains on everyone's enchilada by telling us to stop cos he's got to get up early in the morning. What a killjoy! Let the kids play, man!

Next Door's Cat

Well, that's all from me, dudes! Keep grooving! Why not write down a list of your own top tunes, fave singers and bands below!

Lyrics 2

Danceability 9

Vibes 5

Overall 6

The Collected Memoirs of Ollie Coulton
Part One - The Early Years

As a special treat for you, I have decided to include a small extract from my autobiography *Portrait of a Genius - The Collected Memoirs of Ollie Coulton*. I'm getting the early chapters down now, but I aim to publish it around the time I receive my first Nobel Prize (when I'm about 31).

It's only a first draft. Now and again, I think I come across as a bit too modest, but that's just me - I've always hated showing off.

Preface

Dear reader,

Congratulations on buying/borrowing from the library/listening to an audiobook of *Portrait of a Genius – The Collected Memoirs of* (Sir? Lord?) *Ollie Coulton* (note to editor: add list of awards, doctorates, etc., here).

If you're listening to the audiobook, you'll have noticed that I'm personally narrating it. They haven't gone and got one of these actors who everyone seems obsessed with these days. Why does everyone love actors so much? I fail to see why those playing 'dress-up' and 'pretend' should receive such admiration, when the REAL stars are surely top scientists, mathematicians and incredibly gifted school children.

Where was I?

Yes, my memoirs. For those of you who don't speak French (like Rob), my memoirs are simply my memories. The story of my life. The triumphs and the disasters. Although to be fair, it's mainly triumphs. If you've picked this up to have a good old laugh about the time I spilled an entire pot of yoghurt down my jumper in the school canteen, you'll be disappointed. Minor incidents like this, and the time I accidentally wore my pyjama bottoms to school, or when I was caught talking to my teddy bear, Mr Teddington, will not be repeated here. No one is interested in these things.

Why have I written this book? Well, many times people, including my own friends, have said to me "Ollie, what are you like?" And they've shaken their head with a look of... I think it's admiration mixed with awe. But it's a very good question. What AM I like? Clearly, there is an appetite for knowing more about me and finding out how my (brilliant) mind works.

So, next time I do something that is uniquely and wonderfully 'Ollie Coulton' and someone says "Ollie, what are you like?" I can simply say: "Read the book." Actually, "Buy, THEN read the book." Half the cover price goes towards my crowdfunding project, 'Get Ollie Coulton on Mars by 2025'.

Now, let me take you by the hand, dear reader, as we begin this magical journey...

Chapter 1 – Years 0 - 2

My memory of these years is a little hazy. Vague shapes, colours and, of course, Mr Teddington. So, for an account of my earliest years, I am going to have to rely on reports from my parents. Back in a sec…

I'm back. Well, apparently, I was the most perfect child any parent could wish for. And it was clear, even from my first few weeks, that I was going to be someone very special. My strong voice was singled out for particular praise as, apparently, I would demonstrate its impressive power for long periods, many times a day. Especially when separated from Mr Teddington.

Chapter 2 – Years 2 - 4

My true genius began to show itself in these years. They were a time of considerable achievement. And I was incredibly advanced for my age. For instance, at age two and a half, could inventor of the internet, Tim Berners-Lee get all the different-shaped blocks through the holes in under two minutes? I've checked online and there's no record of him doing so, thus I can only assume he lagged behind me in that department. And could astronaut Tim Peake feed HIMSELF pureed carrot with his own spoon at two years old? Again, there's no evidence of this piece of impressive hand-eye coordination from him. I have much respect for both Tims, but I think both would agree that I was much more advanced than them at the same stage of our lives.

Sorry, Tims! Still a big fan of both of you! - Ollie

Chapter 3 – My First Day at School

Scared, excited, anxious. These were the feelings my teachers must have had when they first met such an amazingly advanced child as me on my first day at school. Would they be able to keep up with my lightning quick powers of reasoning? Three words: no, they wouldn't.

They didn't realise that by age four and a half I already had a reading age of a bright nine-year-old. I had outgrown 'picture' books, with their predictable tales of dogs, balls and brightly coloured objects. Many of these books had no depth whatsoever and their characters were completely two-dimensional (except in pop-up books).

It was during this time that I was unfairly labelled a 'difficult child', because I dared to ask questions nobody else would. Like "Why do I have to do PE," and "Why do I have to go out and play when I want to do more sums?"

It seems I have been asking difficult questions that teachers can't answer all my life…

End of Part One.

NEXT CHAPTER: Why there's nothing childish about bicycle stabilisers.

Brilliant, isn't it?! Easily just as good as Lily's book - and mine is all true!

Dear Angelo's Ice Cream Factory,

Just want to say I'm a HUGE fan of your ice cream. Seriously. It's, like, brilliant. The way you get it so yummy and cold all at the same time is actually genius.

Anyway, I'm looking for a job this summer and I had this brilliant idea. How do you know if your ice cream is definitely yummy enough? What if you were selling not yummy ice cream to people? How would you know?

Fear not, because I've come up with the best solution ever. Three words, guys: Ice. Cream. Taster! That's right! For a very small fee I will spend my summer rocking up to your ice-cream factory and tasting your ice cream for you. Y'know, just to make sure it's definitely properly nice.

What do you think? I can do any day except Wednesdays, cos that's when Sid and I have date night.

Can't wait to hear from you!

Loads of love,
Jas xx

Some of my recent research notes:

Bubblegum ice cream that you can actually blow bubbles with!

Is green really a colour that you want to eat?

You could add some chilli flakes to spice up vanilla ice cream.

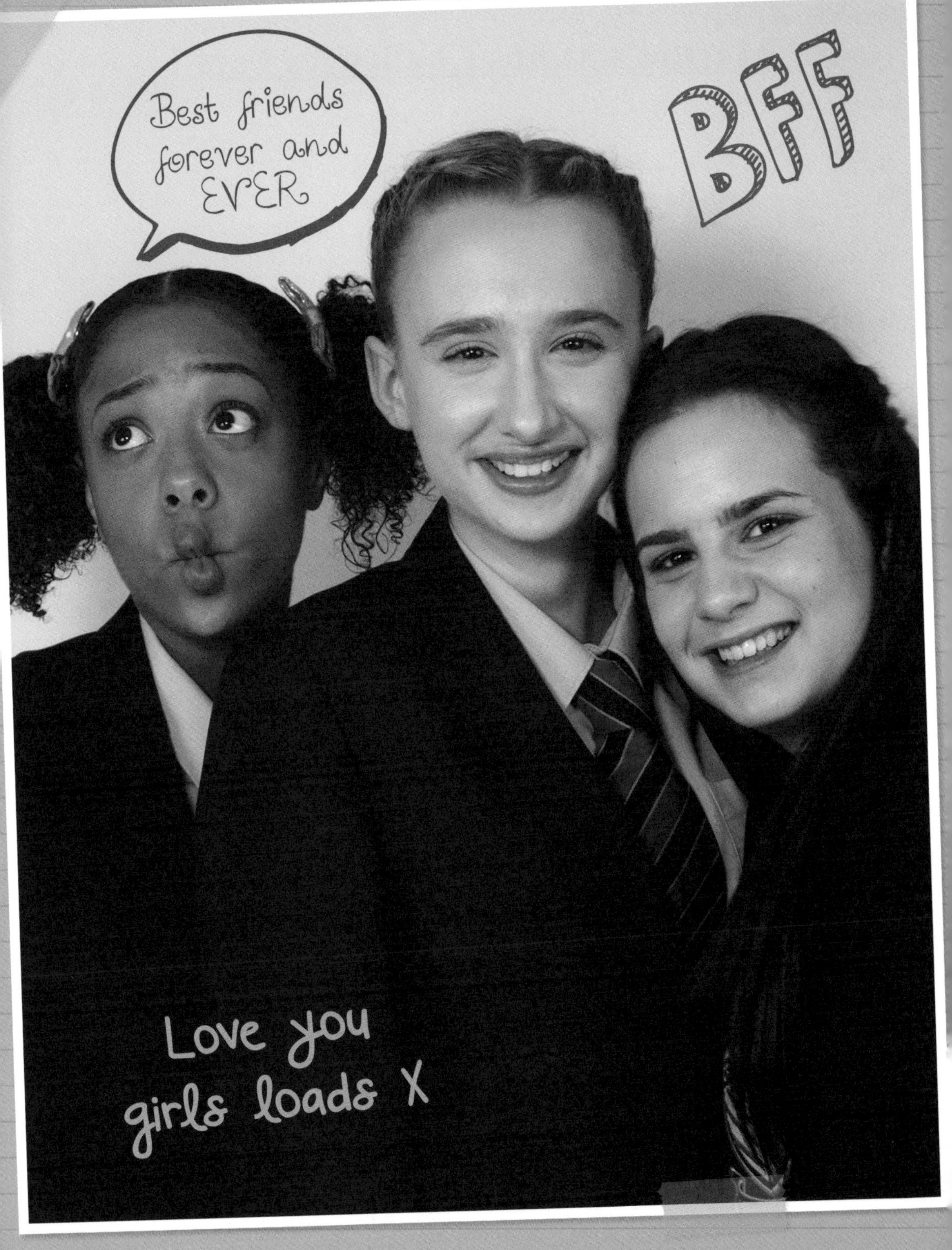
Best friends forever and EVER
BFF
Love you girls loads X

I love to treat myself to some head-scratching maths puzzles.
Below are a few of my favourites:

Martha's Maths Challenges Part 1

1. Trace this shape and cut it out (make sure you cut along the black line into the middle). Crease the folds along all the dashed lines. Now, only folding along the dashed lines, try to fold this shape up into a cube with all six sides covered (some of them can be covered twice, as long as there are no gaps).

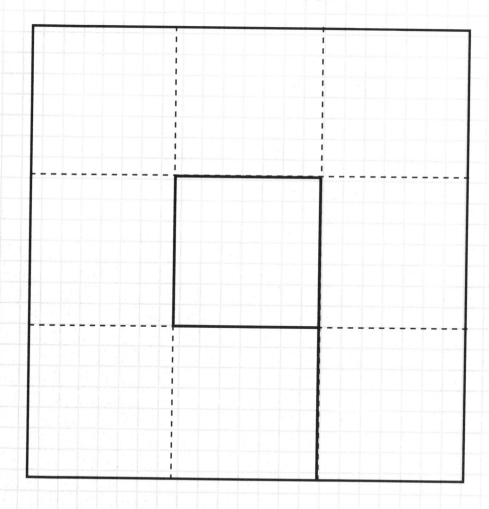

Ollie - I can do this in 2 minutes 34.

Martha - Interesting. I can do it in 2 minutes 30. Not that anyone's counting!

2. Can you draw this house shape without going over any line twice and without lifting your pen off the paper? Start from one of the corners. You should find you can do it starting from some corners but not others. What's special about them?

Once you've got the hang of this one, try drawing your own shapes and challenge your friends to draw them in one go, without drawing over any lines twice. Just don't ask Jas – she always cheats.

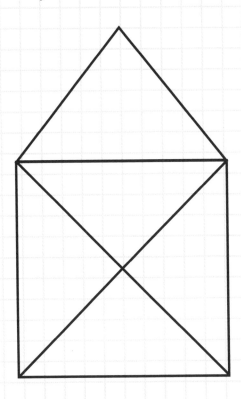

Unfair! I just have a more creative approach than you!

3. Draw a square on a piece of paper. Can you fold up the paper so you can cut out the whole square using one straight cut? What about these other shapes?

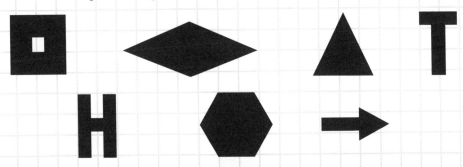

There are even more maths puzzles on pages 148, 149, 178 and 179. If you're really stuck (Jas!), answers are on pages 190-191.

OUR DREAM JOBS

We've realised that people keep asking us what we want to be when we grow up. This becomes a little boring, so we decided to write down a list of ideal professions, so that next time someone asks us this rather unimaginative question, we can simply hand them a list. So, here are our dream jobs:

Lily

* Globe-trotting TV reporter
* Author
* Pop star
* Make-up artist
* Fashion designer
* Interior designer
* Teacher (at good school, NOT Cranmede)

Martha

* Theoretical physicist
* CEO of pharmaceutical company
* Oxford University Professor
* Cambridge University Professor
* Lawyer
(preferably all of the above)

Ollie

1. Astronaut (this is NOT a joke)
2. Famous astronomer
3. Top engineer/computer scientist
4. Professional chess player
5. Billionaire inventor/business magnate like Elon Musk
6. Cambridge University Professor
7. Oxford University Professor

SID

- Activist for world peace/anti-poverty
- Leader of own political party
- Musician
- Head of a charity
- Campaigner for peaceful revolution
- House husband

Jas

+ Inventor
+ Artist
+ TV chef
+ Lifestyle blogger
+ Investigative journalist
+ Dancer/judge on TV dancing show
+ Owner of poorly animal sanctuary
+ Magician

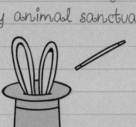

Rob
1. Footballer
2. Football coach
3. PE teacher
   (in that order)

How about you? Write your own list for when someone asks you:

MY DREAM JOBS WOULD BE:

1.

2.

3.

4.

5.

6.

Name of Lesson: THE SPANISH ARMADA	Important: Tuesday is cherry crumble day in canteen – remember to get TWO bowls.
Prepared by: Mr J. Malone, Head of History	
Class: Tuesday, Period 5 after lunch, Year 10	

Time	Activity
	Arrive at classroom – check for cherry crumble stains on tie/ shirt. *Need to check harder - stains v. obvious*
	Thought it was odd when you used this excuse on a day Mrs Griggs was off sick. Enter class and apologise for being late (use excuse 6b – important meeting with Mrs Griggs overran).
	Do register slowly (should use up another 10 minutes). *Always wondered why this was so slow!*
	Do surprise equipment check (should use up another five minutes). *Unbelievable time-wasting!*
	Ask Martha to remind me if there is any homework to collect – if so, collect homework (another five mins gone).
	Check with Martha that we're still doing the Spanish Armada.
	If yes, say, "Right, the Spanish Armada!" If no, ask Martha what we're working on.
	Presuming we ARE doing the Spanish Armada, say, "Who can tell me something about the Spanish Armada? Yes, Ollie?"
	While Ollie drones on and on, get laptop out of bag and search for 'facts about Spanish Armada' (or whatever we're doing) on internet.
	If internet connection down (as per usual), summarise Spanish Armada facts from memory, e.g.:
	• Happened in 1598 *Er, no - it was 1588!*
	• Involved a Spanish fleet of 160 ships *130 ships, actually.*
	• Ordered by King ~~Peter~~ II of Spain *NO! PHILIP II of Spain!!*
	• English was Queen ~~Mary~~ the I *NO! ELIZABETH the I!!!!*
	• Peter II angry that Mary had not punished Sir Walter Raleigh for plundering Spanish ships *Wrong! Sir Francis Drake, NOT Sir Walter Raleigh*
	• Famous Spanish victory
	THE ENGLISH WON!!

Time	Activity
	Get class to read history textbook chapter on Spanish Armada and write down the answers to the questions in silence.

Tell class that while they work in silence, I will perform a role play showing how a Spanish sailor might have slept on board one of the ships.

Take nap until bell.

If someone wakes you before the end of the lesson saying they've finished the work, play *Star Wars* on big screen and say it's based on the Spanish Armada, e.g. Darth Vader is like <u>Peter II</u> and Princess Leia like <u>Mary</u>. PHILIP II IT'S NOT!!!
ELIZABETH I!!!

Set homework: write newspaper article about the Spanish Armada from the point of view of the Spanish or English.

Not this one AGAIN! Must try harder!!

Hello, this is Martha. The above is something I found on the floor of my classroom. It was all crumpled up, lying next to the bin. Scientific curiosity led me to read it and very fascinating reading it was, too! It's a lesson plan written by my history teacher, Mr Malone.

For those of you unfamiliar with lesson plans, these are what all teachers are supposed to do before they teach a lesson, to make sure that the lesson is stimulating and challenging for the pupils, flows logically and results in good learning.

I couldn't help but correct it and return it to Mr Malone, who went bright red and offered me five house points if I never mentioned it again. I said I could not be bought.

Luckily, I had photocopied it before I returned it. Some of you might want to become teachers, so I include this lesson plan as an example of what NOT to do! |

Martha

Chess practice at lunch?

Ollie
It's not on the schedule

I thought we could be spontaneous.

Are you there?

Ollie?

Ollie, please! Answer me if you're there!

Ollie
Sorry. Spontaneity always makes me need to sit down.

I apologise.

Ollie
I'm fine.

No, it was unfair of me. I'll be right over with your breathing bag.

Ollie
Thanks. What time can I expect you?

Sid Bevan

Nicknames: Comrade, Il Maestro, The Dude.

Hobbies: Music, fighting for justice, doing the happy dance with my girlfriend, Jas.

Love is... Like a wave of yes in a sea of why.

In ten years' time I will be... Leading a revolution against the oppressors. Or I might work in a zoo.

Favourite colour: Hope. (Think about it, yeah?)

Favourite quote: 'Hey, Sid, do you want your chips?' – Jas Salford. She's such a profound poet.

If I had a million pounds I would... Redistribute the wealth quickly before I became a cog in the capitalist machine. (I'd probably buy a new speaker system and coffee machine first.)

I couldn't live without... My speaker system and coffee machine.

LILY'S
DREAM DIARY

Sometimes, when I wake up after a dream I think what was that about? So, I've decided to start a dream diary to help me keep track of them and figure out what they mean!

My friends have written their thoughts below, but you might have better explanations!

SCARY NIGHTMARE

Don't read this one if you're easily scared, because it's probably the most frightening nightmare EVER! I'm chilling on the sofa, in my fluffy dressing gown, drinking hot chocolate, when the doorbell rings. I open the door and… it's Rob! He's looking really cute. Like, even cuter than normal, and he's got this sort of shy smile on his face and his eyes are sort of… anyway, he looks cute. I say, "Hi, Rob, what's up?" and he says, "I can't go to the school disco with you – I've got a football match," and I wake up in a cold sweat! Told you it was scary! But what can it mean?

Ollie: You're seriously asking what this dream means? Seriously?

Jas: I think it means, deep down, you secretly want to get a pet dog. And even if it doesn't mean that, I think you should get a pet dog. I could walk it for you! Think about it...

Jas: I'm still picking up a 'wanting a dog' vibe from this dream. It could be a really cute one! Go on! Get one!

ANOTHER ONE ABOUT ROB

I have this one quite a lot. I'm in a church, wearing a white dress and holding a bunch of flowers. Birds are singing and I float down the aisle towards a boy dressed in a nice suit. When I get to the front of the church, I turn around and see that it's Rob! He puts a ring on my finger and looks deep into my eyes and

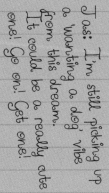

Martha: Okay, I'm stopping this one here because it's making me feel sick.

84

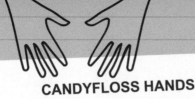

CANDYFLOSS HANDS

I'm in Mr Malone's classroom, but it's not Mr Malone who's teaching, it's TV's Bug Lady Nikita Stricken. I look down and, instead of hands, I've got big balls of candyfloss! I try to tell people, but they just try to eat my hands! I shout at them and then Nikita Stricken tells me that if I keep on shouting she'll put me into her 'naughty bug box'. Then I wake up and – luckily – I don't have candyfloss hands. What's that about?!

Martha: Classic anxiety dream. You want to do well at school but fear something might hold you back. And you were probably watching Nikita Stricken on TV before you went to bed.

Rob: I think you've got a craving for candyfloss and want to go to the fair. Let's go on Saturday!

Jas: I wish I had candyfloss hands!

CAKE SHOP

This is a really random one. I'm walking along the high street, when I see a cake shop and there's a sign in the window saying 'FREE CAKE!' So, I go in and the woman behind the counter says "Would you like some free cake?" So I sit down and the staff keep bringing me cakes: cream cakes, chocolate cakes, cupcakes, birthday cakes...

Jas: Hang on, that's my dream! You stole my dream! Give it back!

Well, that's enough dreams to be going on with. I've got lots more, but most of them have Rob in them.

Why don't you start a dream diary and write down all your dreams? Then your friends can try to work out what they mean!

7 Days to Prepare for Your Exam
By Martha

If you're like me, you're always prepared for exams.

But then there's that one test you forget to input into your digital calendar, you think it's not for weeks, then you check the noticeboard and it hits you...

You have...

7 DAYS TO PREPARE FOR YOUR EXAM.

Day 1

I spend Day 1 calmly planning a study timetable; a detailed plan, allowing time for study, rest, food and recreation.

	MON	TUES	WEDS	THURS	FRI	SAT	SUN	MON
7 A.M.	Wake up early. Eat nutritional breakfast. Mother to quiz me using flashcards.					Wake early. Revise.	Watch *AM Politics*.	Exam day! Wake up early!
8 A.M.	Walk to school. Listen to pre-recorded revision tips while walking.					Brisk walk.	Revise problem areas.	Walk to school.
9 A.M.	Attend lessons. Revise while waiting for Mr M to arrive for register, also during art and PE. Revise during break and lunch with Ollie.					Sit three mock exams.	Late breakfast with Mother.	Exam. Remember to breathe.
3 P.M.	Study with Ollie.	Chess club.	Spanish with Rufus.	Study with Ollie.	Science club.	Mother to mark exams.	Go to town with Ollie.	Review exam with Ollie.
4 P.M.	Walk home. Listen to pre-recorded revision tips while walking.					Check marking.	Select new pen, pencil and eraser.	Begin prep for next exam.
5 P.M.	Dinner and conversation with Mother.					Review exam papers.	Try pre-exam meditation.	Dinner. Review exam.
7 P.M.	Revise Chapter 1.	Revise Chapter 2.	Revise Chapter 3.	Revise Chapter 4.	Revise Chapter 5.	Go to Lily's to 'relax'.	Ensure pencils are sharpened.	Create exam timetable.
8 P.M.	Test on Chapter 1.	Test on Chapter 2.	Test on Chapter 3.	Test on Chapter 4.	Test on Chapter 5.	Go home. Revise.	Early night. Big day tomorrow!	Tidy room = tidy mind.

Then I prepare my nutritious study snacks, download a study playlist and I'm ready to work!

Day 2

I check my study timetable and kick myself! I realise I used the wrong shade of blue on the headings and the lettering is totally the wrong size.
Basically, it's a disaster!
I put the whole thing in the bin and start again...

Day 3

By Day 3 I like to call my friend Ollie for feedback on my study timetable. He helpfully points out any grammatical errors and we spend the rest of the day discussing them.

Day 4

Now it's time for some serious work. I lay out my red pen, black pen, green pen, purple pen and my nutritious study snacks.
I adjust my heater until the room is exactly the right temperature.
I put on my digital watch to ensure I keep to the schedule.
I switch off my phone so no one can interrupt...
Finally, I go to bed exhausted.

Day 5

Wake up in total panic. Cancel everything, plan emergency study timetable and lock door.
Hear buzzing noise. Ignore it.
Take study break to investigate buzzing noise.
After three hours of investigating, I realise it was digital watch.
Throw digital watch out of window.
Spend two hours searching for digital watch in garden.

Day 6

Time to get super serious and search online for study tips!
Discover interesting website.
Realise four hours later that I have spent entire afternoon reading about digital watches. Resolve to stay up all night studying... and immediately fall asleep.

Day 7

Exam day!
Arrive at school unprepared and in a state of panic.
Fall over on way to exam and spend afternoon in nurse's office.
Realise I got the day wrong. My friends tried to call and tell me, but my phone was switched off!

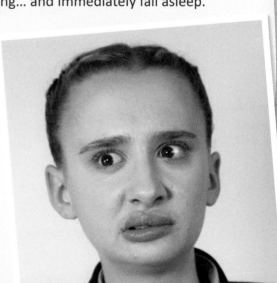

So that's it! Follow my advice and you're guaranteed success! Yeah. Maybe I haven't quite got the hang of this yet.

Ollie's Work Experience Application Letter

Dear Billionaire Inventor and Business Magnate Elon Musk,

Ollie Coulton here. You may have heard of me – I was a quarter-finalist in the UK Youth Chess Championship 2017. I would have done better, but I was coming down with a cold at the time. Or you might be a regular reader of a science blog I write with my friend and colleague Martha Fitzgerald.

In any case, I'll keep this brief, as no doubt you are busy inventing things, checking your stock prices, making speeches, etc.

First, may I say a quick 'well done' for your work in inventing the world's first driverless car. Funnily enough, I had the idea for this years ago – before you, I think! But, sadly, I was too taken up with my other studies to give it my full attention; otherwise, maybe I would be the billionaire and not you!

Anyway, the reason I'm writing is I would like to put myself forward to join the world's first manned mission to Mars that you're working on. I've long had an interest in space exploration and feel I could be a major asset to your team. Things I can offer include:

- Own professional-strength telescope
- Youth (so lots of energy)
- Extreme intelligence (copy of MENSA test results included with this letter)
- High levels of organisation and tidiness (no one wants messy people in space and/or on Mars)
- Excellent personal hygiene (important when sharing cramped spacecraft and/ or Mars colony)
- No occurrence of agoraphobic attacks in over eight weeks

For a character reference please contact Mr J. Malone, care of Cranmede School, England, UK.

I look forward to receiving your reply.

Yours,

O Coulton

Ollie Coulton
PS For spacesuit, I'm a size medium.

KNOW YOUR RIGHTS!
...WITH SID

HOW NOT TO GET PUSHED AROUND BY PREFECTS, TEACHERS, PARENTS AND ANY OTHER WOULD-BE OPPRESSORS!

1 TIDYING YOUR ROOM

Our parent overlords can turn into real STRESS HEADS about the so-called tidiness of our rooms. They fail to realise that the mould in the bottom of a mug is actually an interesting science project. And they don't understand your floor-based filing system for books and papers.

What to do:

Don't actually admit that your room is messy. Say that what with school, after-school activities and dealing with a world full of INJUSTICE, you might have pushed 'tidying your room' (their words) down in your list of priorities. Admit to ONE 'messy thing' (their words again), like a dirty plate or mug. Then deal with that thing alone. Like, wash up the dirty mug. Coming up with a solution and dealing with it will be WELL impressive to your parental units. And it means they might overlook the other stuff!

2 EATING SOMETHING YOU DON'T LIKE

Why are adults always trying to get us to eat stuff we don't like? You could eat a gazillion different things, but say you don't want any broccoli and they act like you've said you want to wear socks on your ears.

Here's some stuff to say when they want you to eat something you don't like. Just replace broccoli with the food that doesn't float your sidecar.

- "I'd love to, but I've given up broccoli for charity."
- "I want to find out what it's like living in a world without broccoli."
- "I'm taking part in an experiment to see what it's like not to eat broccoli."
- "Someone bet me I couldn't NOT eat broccoli and I want to prove them wrong."

3 HAIR NOT BRUSHED

For some reason, letting your hair just do its thing is a big no-no for parents and teachers. Here are some good reasons for not brushing your hair:

- The brush hurts my head.
- I've just used that brush on the dog/cat/hamster/pigeon outside.
- The brush is a present from (name of friend) and they've got nits.

4 SPENDING TOO LONG IN BED

You're having a well-earned Saturday lie-in and you get told to get up! Don't your so-called parents realise you have your BEST IDEAS in bed? Like, I once invented a whole new dance IN A DREAM, so I don't know how anyone can call sleep unproductive. Plus, there's SO MUCH you can do in bed: read, listen to music... even eat! Yes, you MAY get crumbs in the bed. And yes, these crumbs MAY attract ants. But should ants STARVE because of some kind of anti-crumb obsession? I say no! If someone insists you get out of bed, point out that it's SCIENTIFICALLY PROVEN that young people need MORE sleep than anyone else because their bodies are so exhausted from growing and stuff. This is actually TRUE and if they don't believe you, tell them to go and look it up on the internet. That should buy you another ten minutes in bed, anyway.

z z z Z Z Z

5 FAT TIE/THIN TIE

What's the point of ties? Do they serve any purpose? No. And yet our Centres of Oppression (also known as 'SCHOOLS') say that not only do we HAVE to wear them, but also that the knot can't be too FAT or too THIN!!! This totally denies us oppressed workers (or 'school pupils') our INDIVIDUALITY and freedom of expression. Some ideas for fighting this INJUSTICE include:

- Emailing local MP with impassioned plea for a change in school-tie rule.
- Bending rules by having tie a BIT fatter or a BIT thinner than wanted, thus subtly undermining the system.
- Pointing out that your fat tie is in fact a 'Windsor knot' that was popular with KING EDWARD VIII so should be allowed (temporarily suspend disapproval of concept of monarchy).
- Covering tie knot with permanent scarf. Explain wearing scarf indoors using complaint about drafty school classrooms.

I should point out that you can't make the world a fairer place if you're in detention or grounded, so you have to be polite and well mannered at all times when faced with these unreasonable demands. Also, I have come to the conclusion that broccoli is actually quite nice.
STAY STRONG, brothers and sisters!

Your pal, Sid.

Rob

Lily

Hi Rob! How's the holiday so far? Did your plane land OK?

Lily

Hi Rob! You probably didn't get my last message. Otherwise you would have replied! How's it going?

Lily

Wow! You must have really bad reception in Spain. I guess you're not getting ANY of these!

Lily missed call.

Lily missed call.

Lily missed call.

Lily

OK, I checked your flight and it didn't crash, so either you lost your phone or you've met some amazing suntanned Spanish girl and you've decided to live out there forever eating tapas and laughing about me!

Hi Lily. Plane just landed. Weather amazing!

Lily

Great! Bet you wish I was there!

Course I do!

Lily

I mean try not to cry every day. And please don't count the seconds until we can be together again. I know this is hard but you have to be patient. Maybe you could express your feelings in a love poem?

Hahaha! Look at this water slide! I've already been down it 10 times. Then I ate three ice creams! LOL!

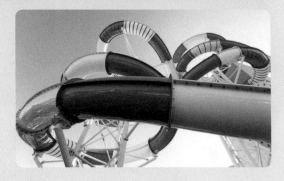

Lily
Right.

Feeling a bit sick actually.

Phew! Made it to the loo in time!

Lily
Glad to hear it! Thanks for sharing, Rob!!! Very romantic. :(

I guess what I'm trying to say is, I miss you.

Lily
Miss you too. I'll let you enjoy your holiday. xxx

Lily
Rob? How much do you miss me?

Martha Fitzgerald

Best friends: Jas, Lily, Ollie, my mother.

Nicknames: Just 'Martha' is fine, thank you.
I get annoyed when people try to give me a nickname.

Hobbies: Astronomy, chess, physics, the pursuit of excellence, cataloguing my book collection with Mother, solving equations with my fellow pursuer of greatness, Ollie.

Favourite chemical element: Vanadium.

Love is...   A hormonal imbalance, easily treatable with fresh air and plenty of water.

In ten years' time I will be...   CEO of my own global tech company, and Nobel prizewinner for physics, chemistry and medicine. If that doesn't work out, my plan is to become the first woman on Mars.

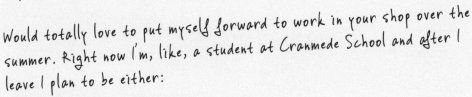

Dear Jake of Jake's Instruments,

Hey man! How's it going?

Would totally love to put myself forward to work in your shop over the summer. Right now I'm, like, a student at Cranmede School and after I leave I plan to be either:

a) a world-famous musician
b) an activist for world peace & anti-poverty

Or maybe combine the two on a rotational basis...

Whichever way you slice the corn dog, I'd deffo be great to have around in your shop cos I sure as trees know my way around all sorts of music-playing things and that. I'm talking guitars (acoustic and electric, twelve string, six string) basses, drums, trumpets, pianos and that one that looks like a big violin... I wanna say... cello??

Anyway, I'd be great and if you wanna maybe leave me on my own with all the instruments while you go and have a nice long lunch somewhere, I'd be totally okay with that.

Let me know!

Cheers, fella,
Sid

Martha and Ollie's Board Game of Excellence

Race your way to success and challenge your wits with our Board Game of Excellence!

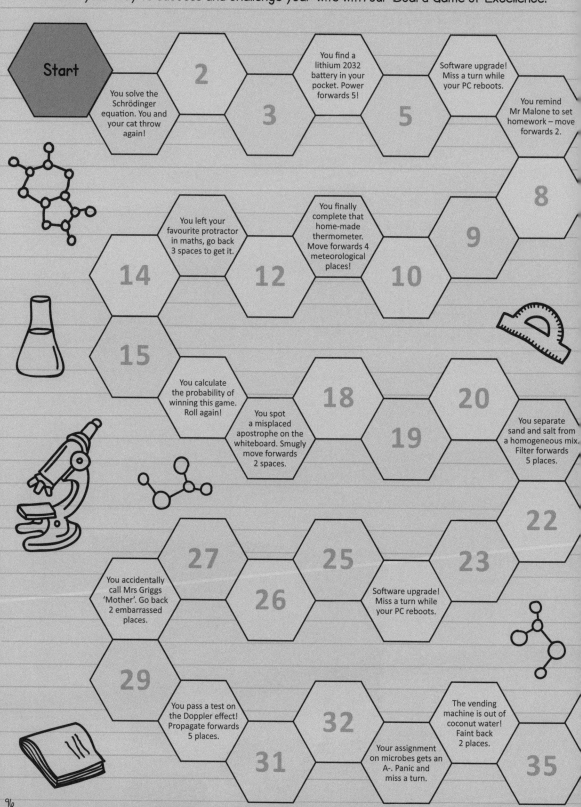

Start

You solve the Schrödinger equation. You and your cat throw again!

2

3

You find a lithium 2032 battery in your pocket. Power forwards 5!

5

Software upgrade! Miss a turn while your PC reboots.

You remind Mr Malone to set homework – move forwards 2.

8

9

You finally complete that home-made thermometer. Move forwards 4 meteorological places!

10

You left your favourite protractor in maths, go back 3 spaces to get it.

12

14

15

You calculate the probability of winning this game. Roll again!

You spot a misplaced apostrophe on the whiteboard. Smugly move forwards 2 spaces.

18

19

20

You separate sand and salt from a homogeneous mix. Filter forwards 5 places.

22

You accidentally call Mrs Griggs 'Mother'. Go back 2 embarrassed places.

27

26

25

Software upgrade! Miss a turn while your PC reboots.

23

29

You pass a test on the Doppler effect! Propagate forwards 5 places.

31

32

Your assignment on microbes gets an A-. Panic and miss a turn.

The vending machine is out of coconut water! Faint back 2 places.

35

You will need

1 die

Counters

For 2 - 6 equally high-minded players.

How to play

1. Cut out these counters.
2. Youngest player starts.
3. Everyone takes turns rolling the die and moving the number of hexagons indicated.
4. Follow the instructions on the hexagon you land on.
5. First player to reach the final hexagon is the winner!

Remember: if you don't win first time around, force your friends to keep playing until you've beaten them.

Finish

Final square. Boys = roll an odd number to win. Girls = roll an even number to win.

63

61

Your proposal to cancel school lunch break is overturned, go back 2 spaces.

60

Discover a new constellation. Roll again... You're nearly there!

54

56

58

You accidentally say something sentimental. Go back 1 humiliating place.

53

57

You find some granite for your rock collection. Polish forwards 2 spaces.

51

49

47

Mr Malone loses your history homework. Go back 3 places to find it.

48

You experiment on kissing without catching anything! Move forwards 2 uninfected places.

Software reboot successful! Roll again!

38

NASA answers your email about bringing your mother into space! Roll again!

You finally spot Lynx in the night sky! Stargaze forwards 5 spaces.

44

You go to see Adam Salt talk about how he dun business. Power forwards 4 spaces.

39

41

43

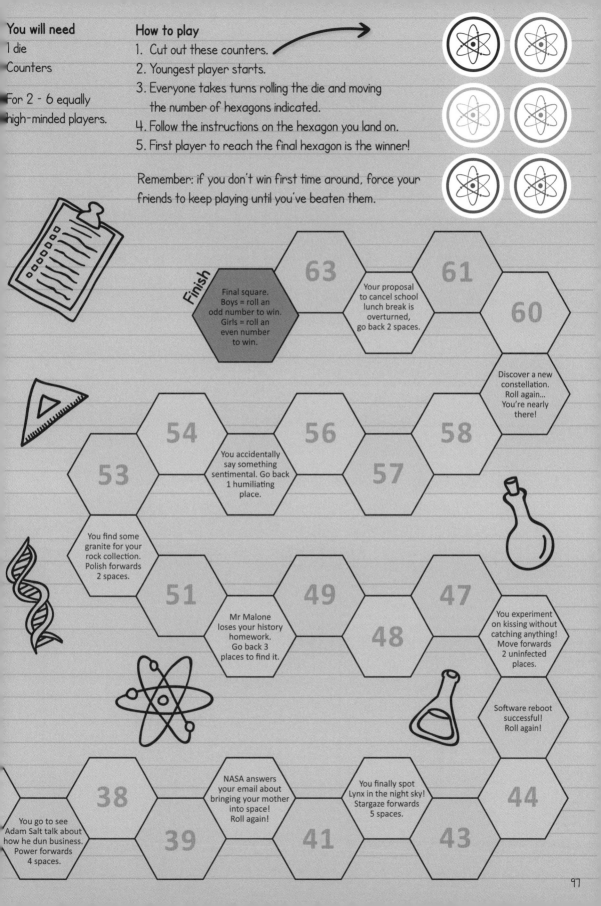

97

Martha and Ollie's Board Game of Excellence
SCOREBOARD

Use this scoreboard to keep track of how many games you've won. Once you've
played enough games you can work out percentage wins - how exciting!

Name of Player	Number of Games Won	Final Position

Dear England Football Manager,

Commiserations on the result of your last match/welcome to your new job (delete the one that doesn't apply).

My name's Rob Edwards and I'd like to be selected for the next international friendly/World Cup/European Championship.

I'm a striker, but I can also play on the wing, so if you need anyone good for either of those positions, I reckon I could be quite handy. And having seen England play recently, you definitely DO need someone good!

Right now, I play for Cranmede School. I've put a list of upcoming fixtures in with this letter, in case you want to send a scout to check me out.

Did I mention, I'm really good? Cos I am!

Cheers,

Rob Edwards

PS My g/f Lily says can she come, too?

TELLY TOAST

BY JAS

You will need:

* Two slices of bread
* Toaster
* Butter or margarine
* Chocolate spread
* Ketchup
* Cheese
* Fudge sauce
* Sprinkles
* One blanket
* One hot-water bottle
  – filled with hot water
* Onesie
* A pair of slippers
* One telly
* One sofa

Method:

1. Put two slices of bread in the toaster. Make sure the dial is set to 4, just crispy enough without burning. Remember the number-one rule, guys: pale-coloured toast is not toast!

2. While the toaster is working its magic you have roughly 4 minutes to get ready. Get your onesie and slippers on and place your hot-water bottle between the blanket and sofa.

3. Get the butter out of the fridge and place it near the toaster so it's just warm enough to spread. Then wait.

4. The second the toaster pops, you have to spring into action. Toast loses its yummy hotness at a rate of one yummy hot per second, so timing is crucial.

5. Use a knife, a spoon, whatever's handy and get that butter on the toast ASAP. Don't worry about making a mess – if you get butter everywhere, you can always lick it off.

6. Squeeze chocolate spread, ketchup, cheese, fudge sauce and anything else you can find onto your toast. Top with sprinkles.

7. If you timed everything right, your hot-water bottle/blanket combo will now be at just the right temperature.

YUM!

Football Coaching for Beginners

by Mr J. Malone,
First Team Coach (acting), Cranmede School
and Rob Edwards, Team Captain

Follow my guide and you can be a brilliant football coach like me! After all, I have a 100 percent win record as football coach of the Cranmede first team.

You were our coach for only one game, though.
And I did help you out with the team talk prematch and at half time, so...?

THE BASICS
Football is a game involving two teams of 11 players, plus the goalkeeper, obviously, making a total of 12.

That's not right, Sir – 11 includes the goalie.

TRAINING
The key to a good training session is bringing the right equipment. Here are some essentials:

- Warm coat, scarf and woolly hat
- Thermos flask (containing hot tea)
- Sandwich
- Throat sweets (because of constant shouting)

Cones?
A football??

Here are some helpful instructions to shout at your players during training:

- "Play better!"
- "Score a goal!"
- "Kick it!"
- "Do football good!"

Keep shouting variations on these key phrases until the quality of football improves.

MATCH DAY
No game is worth risking someone's health over. So if you feel a bit sniffly or tired, don't bother going in. Just text your players with 'Good luck, everyone!'

TOUCHLINE BEHAVIOUR

There's lots you can do to help your team once the match has started, like:

- Starting a chant about how rubbish the opposition are.
- Booing whenever the opposing team have the ball.
- Blowing your own whistle to signal for opposition fouls that the ref has missed.
- If you're winning and the ball goes out of play, holding onto the ball so the opposition can't get it.

DEALING WITH THE REFEREE

Referees appreciate as much help as they can get during the match, so feel free to point out things they might have missed or decisions they might have got wrong.

HALF-TIME

Sometimes there'll be oranges and drinks at half-time, so make sure you get back to the dressing room early to get some of these before the players eat and drink them all.

POST MATCH

There are FIVE possible scenarios at the end of a football match:

1. you win
2. you lose
3. they win
4. they lose
5. you both draw

Are you sure about this, Sir?

Someone once said that the most grown-up and sensible thing to do is to be gracious in defeat and humble in victory. Rubbish! If you win, run around, arms in the air, singing "We are the best, we are the best!" If you lose, feel free to burst into tears and complain about how the result isn't fair.

Happy footballing!!!

For some actually helpful football coaching tips, come and see me, Rob Edwards, at break.

© J. Malone First Team Coach (acting), Cranmede School

Jas's Invention Corner!

Hiya! I'm always inventing things, me. Only problem is, I haven't got time to make them all. So I thought I'd put down the designs here, and if any company wants to make and sell them, they can give me half the money. Deal? Okay, here we go...

THE BEDCAR™

No one likes getting up and going to school. Ease the pain with the BedCar! Simply programme the route to school and at a set time, the BedCar will roll to school and then transform into a chair for learning. At the end of the day, simply climb back into the BedCar and have a much-needed nap on the way home.

Note to designers: this is like a bed with wheels and a satnav. It all automatically folds into a chair – got that?

The MunchBrooch™

Feel sad because you can't manage to eat all your delicious breakfast, lunch or dinner? Simply store the leftovers in your very own MunchBrooch to enjoy later.

Note to designers: so, this is like a sort of wearable lunchbox – easy!

The Bake-o-Wake™

The perfect way to wake up! Add cake ingredients to the Bake-o-Wake, set the timer and get ready to be woken up with delicious, warm cake!!

Note to designers: this would look like a sort of oven with an alarm clock on top and a chute at the back where you pour all the cake ingredients. Also has an extending robot arm that comes out of the oven, holding a baking tray with a cake on it. Couldn't be simpler!

The Auto Stroke 5000™

Too many pets, not enough hands to stroke them? Simply use the Auto Stroke 5000!

Note to designers: what I want here is a sort of frame, with a gap underneath where your pets go. It should have two mechanical arms, with soft gloves on the end of each arm. Oh! And there should be three stroke settings — light stroking, medium stroking and heavy stroking.

The Insta-Tidy™

Are you always getting nagged at for leaving clothes, towels, half-finished plates of food, books, peace-protest banners and designs for inventions all over the floor of your room? Use the Insta-Tidy to instantly remove these items from the sight of parents!

Note to designers: so, imagine, like, strings attached to all the things on the floor leading to a pulley system above the door. When the door gets opened by, for example, your dad, it pulls all the things up to the ceiling out of sight — genius!

Top Tips for the Perfect

♡

Everyone loves a party! Well, except Ollie and Martha, who say they're noisy, chaotic and filled with activities that have no purpose, like dancing. Which brings me to tip number one for the perfect party:

1. No party poopers

When you organise a party you'll always have SOMEONE saying it's a bad idea, like they've got football practice that day. Or they don't like the pirate-fairy theme because they haven't got a thing to wear. Ignore these party poopers and organise the party YOU want!

2. Deal with parents

To avoid embarrassment, you need to lay down some rules for parents to follow, like:

* Absolutely NO dancing
* No singing along to your music
* No putting on 'their' music
* No talking to your friends
* Ideally, stay in a separate room at all times

Party

By Lily Hampton

3. Hide all the embarrassing things

Before you allow your friends, boyfriend or potential future boyfriend in to your house, do a full, forensic-style sweep of the WHOLE area for embarrassing things, like:

* Baby photos
* Childhood paintings stuck to the fridge
* Bravery award for your first visit to dentist that your mum has decided to keep for some reason
* The cuddly toys and teddy bears that you don't even play with/cuddle any more, which just happen to be on your bed because there's nowhere else to put them

After collecting these things, place them at the back of your mum's wardrobe, behind the 10,000 pairs of shoes she never wears.

That's about it - apart from have lots of cake and fizzy drinks! Oh! and remember to invite your friends. I forgot that last one once - v. embarrassing!!

Have a great party!!!

My Hero, SID

I love it when he pulls that face!

Doesn't he have the cutest eyebrows!

MUCK BE GONE LTD

Commercial Cleaning Services Since 1997

"We Love Getting Our Hands Dirty!"

Dear Teacher,

Just a note to let you know how little Ollie got on, doing his work experience at Muck Be Gone Ltd.

Nice lad is Ollie but, to be honest, I don't think he was that happy to be here. Apparently, he applied to do work experience on the International Space Station but didn't get a reply. And as he hadn't got anything else sorted out, he had to come here.

Unfortunately, he wasn't able to do any work on the first day. After I explained what his duties would be (clearing up muck, picking up rubbish, cleaning off dirt, washing off filth and wiping up grime), he fainted and had to go home to recover.

The next day, I didn't even recognise him, as he came in wearing a biohazard suit that covered him from head to toe. The lads all thought it was very funny! And he kept up the joke and didn't take it off all day. Great sense of humour!

To ease him in gently, I sent him to McGinty's farm, as old Mr McGinty needed his largest pig sty given a deep-clean before he turns it into a holiday cottage.

The next day, I received a letter from his mum saying that the whole family had suddenly emigrated to Australia. I hope Ollie enjoys it over there!

All the best,

D BUNCE

Dave Bunce
Manager, Muck Be Gone Ltd

Ollie Coulton Career Plan (TOP SECRET!)

AGE	ACHIEVEMENT	TICK WHEN COMPLETE
18	University: Oxford, Cambridge, Harvard, Princeton or Yale	
21	Graduate with double first	
23	Postgraduate degree at Oxford, Cambridge, Harvard, Princeton or Yale (whichever one I didn't go to at 18)	
26	Complete PhD - insist everyone calls me 'Doctor Coulton'	
27	Take up teaching post at Oxford, Cambridge, Harvard, Princeton or Yale	
28	Win World Chess Championship	
29	Promoted to Professor - insist everyone calls me 'Professor Coulton'	
30	Make major scientific discovery that changes world	
31	Win first Nobel Prize	
32	Take well-earned holiday - on Mars??	
33	Appear on TV's *Pointless* (win)	
35	Publish first volume of memoirs	
36	Win Baillie Gifford Prize for Non-Fiction for memoirs	
37	Discover new star and/or planet and/or galaxy and/or aliens	
38	Marry intellectual equal	
39	Have child genius	
40	Become Fellow of the Royal Society	
41	Invent sequel to internet	
43	Invent teleportation	
45	Finally crack time travel	
46	Go back in time to meet Einstein, Isaac Newton, Marie Curie and Nikola Tesla	
48	Appear on TV's *Mastermind* (win)	
49	Win second Nobel Prize	
50	Big birthday party - let hair down briefly (if still have hair)	
52	Record own album of synthesiser tracks	
53	Synthesiser-tracks album gets to No. 1	
55	Barge holiday on Norfolk Broads	
57	Win third Nobel Prize (suggest it be renamed the Coulton Prize)	
59	Receive knighthood	
60	Retire and devote rest of life to life-changing inventions, breakthrough scientific discoveries and TV quiz show appearances	
?	Donate brain to science/get turned into immortal cyborg	

When I heard Lily was putting together a scrapbook I insisted on submitting some of my favourite recipes!

She tried to talk me out of it, bless her (I think she was worried I wouldn't have time). She even begged me not to submit a recipe and ran away every time I brought the subject up, but I wouldn't take no for an answer!

Below is one of my favourites:

Banana Kipper Hearts by Mrs Hampton

You will need:

Jelly (I like raspberry, but any flavour will do)
Kippers
Old bananas
Cinnamon
Chilli powder
Crushed biscuits
Gravy
Clothes peg

Method:

1. Carefully place the clothes peg over your nose.
2. Mash the bananas, kippers and gravy in a bowl.
3. Carefully shape the banana-kipper mix into 12 little balls.
4. Prepare the jelly in the usual way, then pour the jelly into little heart-shaped moulds.
5. Drop the banana-kipper balls into the moulds.
6. When the jelly has set, sprinkle the crushed biscuits, cinnamon and chilli powder on top.
7. Hey presto! You'll find yourself with a real party crowd-pleaser that also makes a great breakfast treat!

Guys, seriously, please don't try this at home! Kippers, jelly and chilli powder are not a good mix. Take it from someone who knows...

Add your own recipe ideas here!

Martha Fitzgerald Head Girl Speech

(to be used when the inevitable news is announced)
Draft 3 – short version.

(After head teacher introduction, pause to soak up applause and cheering...)

Thank you for your incredibly enthusiastic applause.

(Pause to allow cheering, cries of 'three cheers for Martha', etc., to die down...)

No, really, thank you. Thank you. Please sit down or we'll all be late for our first lesson!

(Pause for laughter...)

Thank you. First, let me say how lucky you are to have me as Head Girl of Cranmede School. Because I will work night and day to be the best head girl there has ever been. And those of you who know me well know that NO ONE works harder than Martha Fitzgerald!

(Pause for cheering and laughter...)

Obviously, I am extremely honoured to be given this position by Mrs Griggs.
(Or name of head teacher if Mrs Griggs has been sacked for erratic behaviour by time of speech.)

As just a very humble, normal, borderline-genius, gifted pupil, I am so surprised to be rewarded with a role of such responsibility.

And I promise you now that I will not let you down.

Under my rule (too much?) **I will begin my campaign of having pointless art, drama and PE lessons removed from the timetable!**

(Pause for cheering...)

And I will not rest until there is extra homework at weekends and an extra hour added to the school day!

(Pause for cheering and chants of 'Martha! Martha! Martha!')

Note to self: be prepared to get carried aloft on pupils' shoulders (take anti-vertigo natural herbal calming remedy).

We love you, Martha!

Martha for HEAD GIRL!

Jas and Sid's
INCREDIBLE
Conspiracy
Theories!!

Life's strangest mysteries SOLVED thanks to the dogged determination of two fearless investigators, who won't REST until they uncover the TRUTH!

Is Mrs Griggs an ALIEN?

Many people have been intrigued by the STRANGE behaviour of Cranmede School's head teacher, Mrs Griggs. We have been watching her closely over a number of months and have come to the conclusion that she is in fact an ALIEN! Observe how she doesn't act like a normal head teacher, seemingly doing NO WORK at all. Then there's the odd way she waggles her fingers when she talks - no HUMAN would ever do this! What about the way she sits cross-legged on her desk making strange 'ohmm' noises? Clearly communicating with her MOTHER SHIP! Pretty conclusive evidence, we're sure you'll agree.

How DID Mr Malone become a teacher?

It's a MYSTERY that no one has been able to solve - just HOW did Mr Malone become a teacher? He seems to know NOTHING about the subjects he teaches. He is RUBBISH at telling people off. We've heard him say he doesn't even WANT to be a teacher! Our theory is that he is actually the SON of Mrs Griggs who, knowing he could never get a job anywhere else, has employed him at Cranmede School, where she can keep an eye on him. And considering we know Mrs Griggs is an ALIEN, that means Mr Malone is an alien, too!

Why ARE Rob and Lily going out?

They are TOTAL OPPOSITES who don't even like the same things. Rob is super sporty, Lily can't catch a ball. They can't get through a week without falling out. SO, the question is, just WHY are they going out with each other??? After a lot of thought, we can exclusively reveal that they are undercover SECRET AGENTS who have been sent to investigate the strange goings-on at Cranmede School, but they are 'chalk and cheese' personalities - one is a maverick who plays by his own rules (Rob), the other is a stick-in-the-mud who does everything by the book (Lily). It all makes sense!

Why are Ollie and Martha NOT going out?

They like EXACTLY the same things. They finish each other's sentences. For our English assignment, where we had to write about our heroes, they wrote about each other. So we have to wonder, why are they NOT going out with each other??? Our current theory is that an eccentric billionaire wants them to invent him a time machine and has promised to fund their research on the condition that they never let a relationship get in the way of their work. Think about it, people! What other explanation could there be???

Where DID the chocolate muffin go?

The strangest mystery we have EVER encountered. We (Jas and Sid) bought TWO chocolate muffins at lunch. Jas ate her chocolate muffin, but Sid was too full up with lasagne to eat his, so we put it in Jas's locker for him to eat later. BUT…! When we went back to get Sid's muffin after school, it was GONE!!! The locker was LOCKED and only JAS had the key, so how could the muffin have disappeared??? Our investigations continue…

The truth is around here somewhere!

MISSING

HAVE YOU SEEN THIS MUFFIN?
LAST SEEN THURSDAY LUNCHTIME

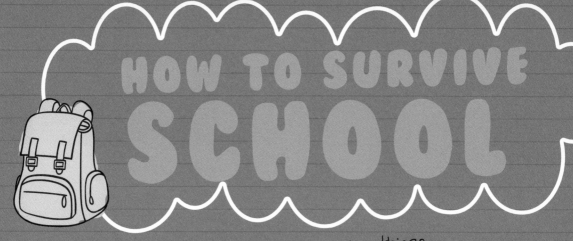

HOW TO SURVIVE SCHOOL

You just have to face it - embarrassing things WILL happen to you at school. When they happen to me, I'm like "Whyyyyy???" and I worry everyone will remember it for, like, ALL TIME.

But, ACTUALLY, I realised from talking to other people that they all just remember the embarrassing things that happened to THEM, not me! So, I guess that's kind of okay!

Lily

It's a loooooong time from first lesson to break, from break to lunch and from lunch to home time. So, have various fruits stashed in your locker in case of hunger attacks.

Jas

Schools are full of germs, so I recommend you carry antibacterial hand gel at all times. However, if you do get a cold, it can be very good for getting out of PE.
Ollie

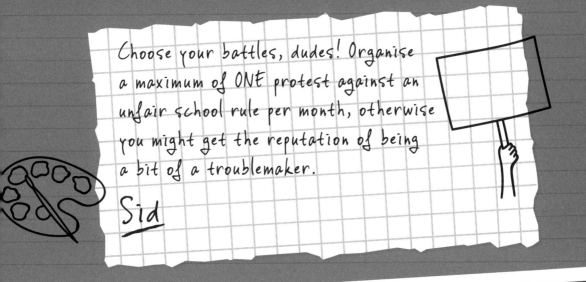

Choose your battles, dudes! Organise a maximum of ONE protest against an unfair school rule per month, otherwise you might get the reputation of being a bit of a troublemaker.

Sid

With compliments

Martha Fitzgerald

You must realise that you will be a lot smarter than some of the teachers. It's not their fault. Try to be kind to them. Point out where they are going wrong quietly rather than letting everyone in the class know. They'll appreciate that.

Martha

People are always asking you questions at school, like what's the square root of whatever and when was the battle of thingy. When this happens, you need to make your eyes go squinty and open your mouth a bit so it looks like the answer is on the tip of your tongue, to give your girlfriend time to whisper the answer to you.

Rob

From: Ferne Hampton
Wednesday 20 May 10.12
Subject: Your Next Star!

Dear Superstars Talent Agency,
I'm writing to ask if you can offer my Lily a summer job as a pop star.
Attached is a photo of her dressed as a tortoise. She really is very, very creative. I've got quite a few pictures like this, so if you need any more, just let me know.
Can't wait to hear from you!
Ferne Hampton

From: Lily Hampton
Wednesday 20 May 11.04
Subject: Re: Your Next Star!

Dear Superstars Talent Agency,
Apologies for the email from my mum. Please ignore her! (Unless you really do think I could be a pop star?! Ha ha, no, I'm kidding. Totally kidding.)
Anyway! If you wouldn't mind, please can you destroy all those photographs of me? Thanks!
Lily Hampton

From: Ferne Hampton
Wednesday 20 May 11.20
Subject: Shy

Dear Superstars Talent Agency,
Please ignore Lily's last email telling you to ignore my email. She's just being shy! Honestly, she's a great little singer. She makes up these sweet little songs about her boyfriend in the shower – you should hear them!
Ferne Hampton

From: Ferne Hampton
Wednesday 20 May 13.04
Subject: Don't Listen to My Lily

Dear Superstars Talent Agency,
My daughter has just (slightly rudely) informed me that she doesn't make up songs
in the shower and I have to stop telling people she does.
To be honest, I think she's just a bit worried that we're coming across as a bit
strange, when obviously nothing could be further from the truth, right?
Anyway, more photos attached!
Ferne x

From: Lily Hampton
Wednesday 20 May 13.15
Subject: Re: Don't Listen to My Lily

Mum!
Stop emailing photos of me wearing pants on my head to strangers!!!!
Lily

From: Caroline Mills
Monday 25 May 14.46
Subject: Please Read Carefully

Dear Lily/Mrs Hampton,
Many thanks for your emails, which I have finally had the chance to read.
Please be aware we don't actually represent pop stars, we're an animal talent agency.
May I suggest you talk to each other instead of sending each other weird emails?
And please, please stop including me in this. I've got an agency to run.
Yours sincerely,
Caroline Mills
Superstars Talent Agency

From: Ferne Hampton
Monday 25 May 15.23
Subject: Re: Please Read Carefully

Dear Lily,
Well, that sounded like a definite maybe! Want me to reply?
Love Mum x

To CERN,

I am writing to enquire if I may be considered for a summer position at the Large Hadron Collider this summer.

I had hoped I could work for NASA, but they didn't reply to any of my emails, so you are my second choice. But don't worry, I'm sure we can all make the best of it.

I have no formal experience of working in particle acceleration as such; however, I am a straight-A student with a commitment to excellence in the field of nuclear science and astrophysics. Please find attached my 326-point plan on how I can improve CERN during my time with you. To summarise, I shall:

- Submit all personnel to a rigorous aptitude test. (Anyone scoring less than 98 percent would, of course, be fired.)
- Enlist my friend Ollie to upgrade your IT systems.
- Make my mother a permanent member of the executive board (she has a few ideas of improvements of her own, which she will contact you with in due course).
- Reorganise the stationery cupboard.

All thoughts welcome, although Mother and I will of course have the final say on whatever improvements we carry out.

I think that's everything for now. I look forward to hearing from you.

Yours in anticipation,

Martha Fitzgerald

Martha Fitzgerald

PAMPERED PET PAWS GROOMING PARLOUR

WE'RE THE DOG AND
CAT'S BEST FRIEND!

Dear Mr Malone,

It was lovely to welcome Jas into our little dog-grooming parlour for her work experience last week. She's a real credit to your school, so full of enthusiasm and imaginative ideas!

Some of her ideas were a little TOO imaginative. Like leaving the dogs in the bath to wash themselves while she went to Big Sam's Sandwich Bar for an extended lunch break. Or the idea of letting the dogs into the cat section so that they could all 'play together'. That caused a bit of a kerfuffle, I can tell you!

The only other slight mishap was when Jas mistakenly took a delivery of hair dye meant for the hairdressers' next door and it got mixed up with our doggy shampoo, meaning that all the dogs got dyed blue. But she was very good at convincing the owners that ALL dogs were going blue this season.

Eventually, Friday came and, sadly, we had to say goodbye to Jas. She did ask if she could maybe come and work here on Saturdays, but I had to tell her that we were fully staffed and that it would be absolutely IMPOSSIBLE for her to do so.

By the way, in case you're thinking of popping by, the grooming parlour will be closed next week while I go on holiday to recover.

Yours sincerely,

J Butterworth

Janice Butterworth
Owner

From: F.Fitzgerald@CGILtd.co.uk
Tuesday 13 September 10.07
Subject: Work Experience

Dear Mr Malone,

I believe I am obliged to write a follow-up appraisal of Martha's work experience week.

As you know, Martha chose to spend her work experience at City Global Investments Ltd. And, as both Martha's mother AND the CEO of CGI Ltd (UK division), I was very happy to welcome her.

It was quite tricky to fit her into the company, considering we are fully staffed and I HATE overstaffing. But, luckily, after I fired my personal assistant, Martin, a suitable vacancy became available.

Suffice to say, Martha EXCELLED in her position. In as little as five days, she had impressed the other directors so much that she was offered a place on the board and began restructuring the entire company.

I was so proud to see her at work. And I was extremely impressed when she identified that the company would be best run by merging the UK division with our sister company in the US, resulting in me losing my job. It's this kind of cold-hearted ruthlessness that makes a mother's heart swell!

Luckily for me, Martha returned to school just in time for me to do some hasty bribing of the board and take over as head of the company again. Which meant I could give Martin his job back and stop him phoning me at all hours to cry.

Winners all round!

Sincerely,

F. Fitzgerald
CEO CGI (UK) Ltd

Sent from my smartphone

Form 5M History Field Trip Report
By Lily Hampton

8 a.m. Form 5M and Mr Jeff Malone board coach for Warwick Castle.

8.15 a.m. Coach still hasn't left school car park.

8.20 a.m. Martha Fitzgerald reminds Mr Malone he is supposed to be driving.

8.25 a.m. Coach sets off for Warwick Castle. Lily Hampton had, cleverly, brought napkins and candles for romantic breakfast date with Rob Edwards.

8.26 a.m. Martha Fitzgerald attempts to confiscate romantic breakfast, insisting "We're here to learn!"

8.30 a.m. Ollie Coulton announces he's feeling travel sick. Unfortunately, Lily and Martha are too busy arguing about the picnic to hear.

8.35 a.m. Ollie throws up all over Lily's romantic napkins.

10.00 a.m. Warwick Castle looks amazing in the morning sun! Form 5M, however, do not get to see this; they spend the morning driving around Warwick because Mr Malone refuses to ask for directions.

12 p.m. Form 5M finally arrive at castle. Lily Hampton tries to wander around, soaking up romantic atmosphere with Rob Edwards. Unfortunately, Jas Salford makes everyone stop for lunch.

12.15 p.m. Lily Hampton tries to create romantic lunch with napkins and candles.

12.20 p.m. Jas Salford knocks candles over and nearly sets fire to 200-year-old curtains.

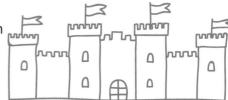

12.30 p.m. Ollie Coulton announces he still feels sick. Mr Malone tells him to stop complaining.

12.40 p.m. Ollie is sick on Mr Malone's shoes.

12.45 p.m. Sid and Jas Salford re-enact the Battle of Edgehill using swords from the gift shop. Mr Malone forced to intervene.

12.50 p.m. Sid and Jas Salford start an anti-war protest on castle ramparts. Mr Malone forced to intervene.

1.15 p.m. Martha Fitzgerald starts protest against the imprisonment of Joan of Arc. Mr Malone tried to intervene but told to sit back down again by Martha Fitzgerald.

1.30 p.m. Martha, Sid and Jas force manager of Warwick Castle to apologise for all social injustice.

1.45 p.m. Manager of Warwick Castle forces Mr Malone to apologise for behaviour of pupils.

1.50 p.m. Martha Fitzgerald and Ollie Coulton present manager of Warwick Castle with a list of all factual inaccuracies they have identified in the castle guidebook.

1.52 p.m. Martha Fitzgerald and the manager of Warwick Castle enter into heated debate about castle guidebook.

1.55 p.m. Martha Fitzgerald calls her mum for legal representation.

1.55 p.m. and 30 seconds Manager of Warwick Castle forced to admit Martha was right, promising to reprint guidebook with Martha and Mrs Fitzgerald's full editorial approval.

2 p.m. Martha Fitzgerald notices Mr Malone is missing.

2.30 p.m. After thorough search coordinated by Martha Fitzgerald and Ollie Coulton, Mr Malone discovered hiding in medieval suit of armour in castle dungeons.

2.40 p.m. Despite begging, flattery and bribery from Jas Salford, Martha Fitzgerald, Lily Hampton and castle manager, Mr Malone refuses to come out from inside medieval suit of armour.

2.45 p.m. Rob Edwards agrees to stay with Mr Malone until he's feeling better. Lily Hampton gives up all hopes of a romantic day out.

3 p.m. Lily Hampton finally loses temper and yells at everyone to get back on the coach.

3.02 p.m. Everyone gets back on the coach.

3.15 p.m. Coach still hasn't left castle car park.

3.15 p.m. Martha Fitzgerald again reminds Mr Malone he is supposed to be driving.

3.30 p.m. Lily and Rob have romantic moment on coach when Rob gives Lily a Saxon bracelet he bought in the gift shop.

3.35 p.m. Lily Hampton decides school trips aren't so bad, after all.

3.45 p.m. Ollie Coulton is sick on bracelet.

Ew! Gross!

I forgot my travel sickness tablets. Sorry, Lily!

Greetings from Warwick Castle!

JASICTIONARY

I just LOVE made-up words. You know, those nonsense words you make up for fun and only your friends know what they mean. I'm thinking of starting my own dictionary. Here are a few of my favourites:

Barp That noise you make when you think you're going to burp but then you swallow it but then it comes out anyway.

Yumghurt One of those yoghurts with the chocolatey bits that are so yum they're technically too nice to be a yoghurt but they are still in the yoghurt aisle of the supermarket.

Notfall That thing when you fall over but stop yourself at the last minute.

Marthglare That look Martha gives you when she's trying to work but you're trying to show her the new move you learned in interpretive dance class.

Fluffmint That sweet you find in the bottom of your bag that isn't technically safe to eat but it's one of your favourites, so you blow the bits off and eat it anyway.

Breakfall That thing when you fall over, but stop yourself at the last minute, but accidentally break something anyway.

Snack Snack Break Break A break where you stop for a snack in the middle of eating a snack.

Happisnug That feeling you get when your boyfriend, Sid, smiles. Or when your boyfriend, Sid, wipes butter off his nose. Or when your boyfriend, Sid, saves you a button for that sock puppet you're making.

Disastrophe A total, total nightmare situation. Like when someone's had the last triple choc chip on canteen muffin day.

Aw thanks, Jas!

Add your own made-up words and definitions here and I'll include them in my Jasictionary!

Martha and Ollie's Science Experiment

Aim	To discover whether or not Rob and Lily can go an entire school week without falling out over some trivial matter.
Prediction	They will DEFINITELY fall out over some trivial matter at some point within school hours across a five-day time period (40 hours precisely).
Explain why you think this will happen	Newton's third law states that every action has an equal and opposite reaction. So when Lily, for example, suggests to Rob that they go shoe shopping for two hours, he will inevitably suggest they do exactly the opposite action (like watch a football match on television) for an equal amount of time.
Apparatus	1 x Rob 1 x Lily 1 x binoculars 1 x notepad 1 x ballpoint pen Sandwiches Coconut water
Method	By following Rob and Lily as they went about the school day, we were able to observe how well they were getting on, at hourly intervals. One of us would observe, while the other would use a simple graph system of smiley faces or sad faces to monitor the state of their relationship. In the event of being told to 'go away' or to 'stop spying on us', we would retreat to a safe distance and observe them via Ollie's professional-grade field binoculars. A steady supply of sandwiches and coconut water provided necessary sustenance throughout the duration of the experiment.

Data

This is what we observed:

	MON	TUES	WEDS	THURS	FRI
8.30-9.30 A.M.	:)	:)	:)	:)	:)
9.30-10.30 A.M.	:)	:)	:)	:)	:)
10.30-11.30 A.M.	:)	:)	:)	:)	:)
11.30-12.30 P.M.	:)	:)	:)	:)	:)
12.30-1.30 P.M.	:)	:)	:)	:)	:)
1.30-2.30 P.M.	:)	:)	:)	:)	:)
2.30-3.30 P.M.	:)	:)	:)	:)	:(
3.30-4.30 P.M.	:)	:)	:)	:)	:)

Results

Rob and Lily were getting on really well all through the week and then, at 3.04 p.m. precisely, Lily noticed Rob 'getting on really well' with Jenny Jones in the library. Lily sulked for exactly 23 minutes, ignoring Rob's request to 'tell me what's the matter'. Eventually, Lily confessed to observing 'long in-depth chat' with Jenny Jones, but Rob explained that Jenny was simply explaining the plot of the novel *Wuthering Heights*, so that Rob didn't have to read it. Rob and Lily then proceeded to make up, with apologies and talking to each other in yucky cooing voices. Ugh!

Conclusion

It has been proven conclusively that Rob and Lily are UNABLE to go an entire school week without falling out over some trivial matter. QED.

Rob and Lily are a scientific anomaly. Perhaps love cannot be explained by science.

Mr Malone, I have a spare guitar strap if you need it? - Sid

It's not what I'd choose to listen to, but good for you! - Lily

Dear Derek Leatherhair,

Hey, Dezza! Singer-songwriter Jeff Malone here.

You may have heard my debut album *Malone Alone* – a collection of wistful yet powerful acoustic guitar ballads. Here are some reviews for the album:

'Wistful yet powerful acoustic guitar ballads.'
- Official Press Release

'Original… surprising and unusual.'
- Sid, Yr. 10

'I'm afraid we cannot accept unsolicited submissions.'
- BPJ Music Inc.

A mixed bag review-wise, but works of genius are often unappreciated in their own time.

Anyway, as one musician to another, I would like to put myself forward to join your band, Leatherblare.

I know members of your group keep leaving, saying that you're bossy and impossible to work with, but I think they're just jealous of your talent. If I were your new rhythm guitarist, I would know my place and only speak when I'm spoken to! Plus – I'm your No.1 fan. I've got all your albums and I've been to see you 28 times, so I know how all the songs go already!

Unfortunately, owing to my commitments as a secondary school teacher, I can only tour between July and September. Although I may be able to do the odd day at other times by taking a sickie. Have guitar, will rock!

Sincerely,

J Malone

Jeff Malone

PS Please find enclosed a CD of my latest album, Malone Alone, enclosed as evidence of musical talent and skill.

PPS You don't need to pay me or anything!

PPPS PLEASE! I need this! Being a teacher is dead boring!!!

Z Z Z Z Z

I think I'd rather forget it! - Rob

Lily, wasn't this after one of your arguments with Rob? - Jas

Rememeber this amazing science lesson! - Martha

Jas here! I found these at the back of a book Rufus lent me – they're some amazing poems he's written! Obviously, he'd LOVE to see them in print, so I put them in our scrapbook as a brilliant surprise! You're welcome, Rufus!!

Dream Girl

Dream girl holds her test tube
I wish she would hold me
Dream girl understands biophysics
But does she understand me?
Dream girl knows the formula
To Newton's famous law
But does she even notice
When I walk through the door?
No.
Dream girl, I dream you're in my arms
Will my dream come true? I hope!
But now you're at his house again
Looking through his telescope.

Cool Kid

See the blue-eyed Cool Kid
With his coconut water
Hope someone takes him down a peg
Someone really oughta!

He's so smug and cocky
Hear his triumphant laughter!
Just because he's going out
With clever, lovely Martha.

Cool Kid wants to go to Mars
In spite of all the danger
Go then, Cool Kid! Leave your love
With the Spanish-speaking stranger.

Te Amo

'Te amo' means 'I love you'
In the language of Spanish
'Ser mío' means 'be mine', my love
Oh, I wish that we could vanish
Away from here, away from him!
And his ~~face~~ ridiculous good looks
Though after a while you'd probably miss
Your chemistry textbooks.
But who needs chemistry, anyway
When we have Spanish learning?
Let me teach you the subjunctive tense!
Oh, Martha, hear my yearning!
One day you would forget him
And you'd say 'te amo', too
There'd be no pesky Ollie
To come between me and you.

LILY'S GUIDE TO
AN-GRRRR MANAGEMENT

Obviously, I never lose my temper.
OK, fine, maybe I lost it once, like, ages ago.

FINE, OK! I LOSE MY TEMPER SOMETIMES! STOP GOING ON ABOUT IT!!!

A-hem. What I mean is, getting angry is perfectly normal and everyone does it.
My friends call it 'The Full Hampton' because when I go, I completely lose all control. Ever have that feeling?

Good luck!
Love Lily x

Know the signs!

You know the feeling. Your heart speeds up, you grit your teeth, maybe clench your fists. Learn to spot when you're about to go 'Full Hampton'. What makes you angry? Unfairness? Fear? Once you know the ~~the~~ triggers, it's easier to take action...

Breathe!

Count to 10, list your favourite songs and then find five things in the room beginning with S. Just take yourself out of the moment. Then, when you feel like you again, just step right back in!

Write it down

Anger is often mixed up with other feelings: sadness, frustration, worry. Keep a diary, draw a picture, express yourself! Figuring out what's causing those feelings will help to manage them.

Get physical

Exercise makes your brain release happy chemicals that leave you feeling great for ages afterwards. Don't worry if you're not the best or the fastest - the best exercise is the kind you do for yourself, because it gets that anger out there in a safe, healthy way!

Need some extra help?

Talking honestly and calmly with the people you trust is a great way to figure things out. If you're struggling with your feelings, you're just like millions of other people who need a bit of extra help sometimes. Talking treatments, books and anger management courses can be massively helpful. You can ask a doctor or school councillor what might work for you.

Form 5M: *Summer Timetable*

MONDAY	TUESDAY	WEDNESDAY	THURSDAY	FRIDAY
History	Science	PE	Double Art	Geography
Martha to provide Mr Malone with lesson plan.	Note to self: replace broken test tube, Bunsen burners and flask. Also, find new way to make cup of tea in chemistry – Jas	Don't forget excuse note from Mum – Lily	Otherwise known as double 'Total Waste of Time!' Jas to replace my broken easel from last week.	Oooh! geography! With Little Miss Perfect. Sir! It's spelt 'Parfitt'. We've been through this!

LUNCH ★ ★ ★ ★ ★ ★ ★ ★

Chess Club	Debating Society	History Club		Band Practice
Read out Code of Conduct to new members and weed out the time-wasters!	This week's topic of debate: Rights for Germs! Is cleaning murder?	Lily to remind Mr Malone to turn up this week.	Lasagne day!!! Be 1st in lunch queue.	If Mr Malone asks, tell him Sid's on litter duty. – Jas

Double Maths	Music	Double English	PSHE	French Test
Ollie and I to present research on cubic equations... quickly, before anyone can stop us. 	Remember to bring didgeridoo. Also, remember to learn to play didgeridoo.	Read out extracts from *Hero of the Hour*. I just hope everyone's ready for it! - Lx	If you need me, I'll be hiding in the library - Martha	*Facile! Je connais le chapeau de singe.* 'I know the monkey hat'? Lily, I think your translator app is broken again! M x

AFTER SCHOOL

Martha to meet Ollie for extra study.	Martha to meet Ollie for phone synch Tuesday. **Cowboy Karaoke night!!! Love Mrs H #xxx** Thanks, Mum! :) Lx	Martha to meet Ollie for loads of snogging. Jas! Cross that out!	Lily to meet Rob for casual date. Absolutely no big deal - it's just casual. PLAN TEN OUTFITS! DON'T BE LATE!	Jas and Sid sponsored hop for charity. Save The Ants. Be there or be our ant-hating loser! 

Ollie's Rorschach Test

A Rorschach test, invented by a psychologist called Hermann Rorschach (pronounced 'raw-shack'), is where you look at random blobs and say what they remind you of. Some people say this can tell you about your personality.

In the spirit of science, I have decided to run my OWN Rorschach test! Why not ask your friends what they can see?

Lily: Ooh, it's a butterfly!

Martha: I don't understand. It looks like a blob of ink.

Rob: I'm going to go with a bug. No, a squashed bug!

Jas: It's obviously a drizzle of delicious salted caramel sauce.

SID: I can see peace, love and hope for the world.

Lily: It's a face!   Martha: It's... another blob of ink.

Jas: It's a cake with a face on it?

SID: Personally, I see the face of all the oppressed peoples in the world.

Rob: It's the scary clown from my nightmare! Get it away!

Lily: Easy - Christmas tree!

SID: I see a flag for a new nation built on fairness and equality.

Martha: What's with showing me all these blobs of ink, Ollie? What are you trying to achieve, exactly?

Rob: I can still see the scary clown from my nightmares! It's there every time I close my eyes! What have you done, Ollie?!

Jas: Hmm, not sure, but for some reason I can taste mince pies.

Lily: Hmmm... not sure about this one... it looks like... the cake I dropped on the floor that time. That was so embarrassing.

Martha: Oh, OK, I think I'm getting the hang of this now! Yes! I see... a crab and a jellyfish dancing a tango. Is that it?

Ollie: Oh, sorry, this is actually just some spilled ink that I was blotting up earlier. Don't know how that got in there. Ignore that one.

Martha: This test is stupid.

Aaargh!
Scary clown again!

At this point, the Rorschach test was abandoned while Lily tried to get Rob to stop screaming. Martha refused to take part any more, saying the test proved absolutely nothing. And Jas said the test had made her hungry so left for Big Sam's Sandwich Shop, taking Sid with her.

Oh well, a fascinating experiment, I'm sure you'll agree! So, does the Rorschach test tell us anything about someone's personality?
The results are inconclusive.

PROUDEST MOMENTS

I asked everyone to tell me the proudest moment of the year. Here's what we came up with!

Outstanding Achievement
in PHYSICS
is awarded to

Martha Fitzgerald

Signed ..... *Mrs Griggs*

Outstanding Achievement
in MATHEMATICS
is awarded to

Martha Fitzgerald

President of
Astronomy Club

Martha Fitzgerald

MARTHA

I have so many, I couldn't choose my favourite! Could I maybe get another page?

♡ **Ollie Coulton** ♡

is hereby recognised for his contribution in the

field of snogging

Which he is totally brilliant at and I should know, I've snogged him loads.

Signed .... *Martha*

Ollie

Oh, very funny, Jas! You'd better not let Martha see this!

Go Team Cupcake!

Winner of the Polymathalon Cup.

Martha - I think you'll find team Big Bang won this year.

Ollie - Guys, we switched teams?
You both won it, remember?

Cranmede School Bake-Off

2nd Prize is awarded to

Jas Salford

For her imaginative Fish Finger and Chocolate Cake. With bonus prize for only eating half of it before the contest was over.

Signed _____*Mrs Griggs*_____

Aaah, fish, breadcrumbs, chocolate - what's not to love?

Martha's Maths Challenges Part 2

1. These nonogram puzzles have hidden pictures! The numbers by each row and column tell you how many squares in that row or column are coloured in in the finished puzzle and each number represents a solid block of that size. If there's more than one number, the blocks have to be separated by at least one blank square.

You can use a small x to mark squares you know definitely aren't coloured in. Can you complete them and find the finished picture?

Hint: for the first picture, think about where the blocks of eight will have to be; for the second picture, try filling the fourth row...

```
          0  3  6  7  7  7  7  6  3  0
       0
   2   2
       8
       8
       8
       6
       6
       4
       2
       0
```

```
                        1  1        1  1  1
                        1  2  1  1  1  1
                     1  2  2  2  1  1  2  1
                  6  1  1  1  1  1  1  1  1  6
           6
      1    1
   1  1    1
1  2  3    1
      1    1
1  1  1    1
   1  6    1
   1  2    1
      1    1
           6
```

148

You can also use this blank grid to make your own puzzle – fill in some squares, work out the numbers around the side and give a blank grid to a friend.

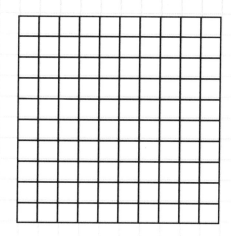

2. Be a pizza detective! Three unlabelled pizza boxes are in a stack. If the pepperoni pizza is above the Hawaiian pizza and the Hawaiian pizza is below the veggie pizza, which of these statements are true?

A. The veggie pizza is on the top
B. The Hawaiian pizza is at the bottom
C. The pepperoni pizza is in the middle
D. The pepperoni pizza is on top
E. None of the above
F. Jas will eat all the pizza as a reward for being awesome

Jas! You are disrespecting maths!

And here I was thinking you were disrespecting pizza

3. Can you cut a cake into eight pieces making only three straight cuts?

Go on then Jas, make a 'cake' joke, I know you want to!

I can't. I'm still full from the pizza!

If you loved these puzzles and want to do more, turn to pages 76, 77, 178 and 179. Check your work on pages 190 - 191.

Minutes of meeting to decide the theme for Cranmede School's Charity Non-Uniform Day

Location of meeting: Mr Malone's classroom   Time of meeting: Thursday lunchtime

Present at the meeting: Present (but late):   Not present at the meeting:
Martha   Lily   Everyone else in the class
Ollie   Rob   (even though they were
                               Jas   supposed to come).
                               Sid
                               Rufus
                               Jenny Jones
                               Mr Malone

Designated taker of the meeting's minutes: Martha Fitzgerald.

12.30 p.m. – Meeting begins. Only Martha and Ollie present, despite everyone knowing that the meeting was supposed to start at 12.30 p.m. on the dot.

Martha suggests that everyone's lateness reflects very poorly on them. Ollie agrees and suggests they begin without them.

Martha agrees and announces purpose of meeting: to decide the theme of Cranmede School's charity non-uniform day.

Ollie expresses excitement that finally it is the turn Mr Malone's class to choose the theme of the non-uniform day, after the highly disappointing and embarrassing previous themes chosen by other classes – most ghastly of all being 'superheroes'.

Martha agrees and suggests that if the others can't be bothered to turn up on time, they shouldn't be allowed to have an input. Ollie agrees.

Lily and Rob arrive at meeting. Ollie points out that they are late.

Martha repeats the purpose of the meeting for the benefit of Lily and Rob: to decide the theme of Cranmede School's charity non-uniform day.

Rob makes a suggestion for the theme of the non-uniform day: 'superheroes'.

Ollie makes sort of groan/sigh noise.

Rufus and Jenny Jones arrive. Ollie points out that they are late.

Martha repeats the purpose of the meeting for the benefit of Rufus and Jenny Jones: to decide the theme of Cranmede School's charity non-uniform day.

Rob repeats his suggestion: 'superheroes'.

Jenny Jones remarks that 'superheroes are so in right now'.

Ollie points out that the school has already done the theme of superheroes.

Rob remarks 'So?'. Remark is ignored.

Martha puts forward a suggestion: everyone should dress as their favourite physicist. Rufus and Ollie agree.

Rufus requests the record show that he thinks Martha's suggestion is 'brilliant'.

Martha asks for a show of hands in support of the motion.

Results: three in favour (Ollie, Martha, Rufus) and three against (Lily, Rob, Jenny Jones). Stalemate.

Jas and Sid arrive. Ollie points out that they are late.

Martha repeats the purpose of the meeting for the benefit of Jas and Sid: to decide the theme of Cranmede School's charity non-uniform day.

Jas makes suggestion: 'superheroes'.

Ollie goes red and forcefully informs those present that the school has already done the theme of superheroes.

Ollie goes on extended rant about importance of turning up on time to meetings.

Jas suggests that Ollie might like to 'cool his jets'.

Ollie apologises and makes a request for his remarks to be struck from the record. Martha refuses his request, saying the record must show a true account of the meeting.

Ollie starts sulking.

Martha suggests that they have another vote for her 'famous physicists' idea. Rufus agrees with Martha.

Ollie suggests there's no point as they have already voted and it is highly unlikely everyone else will go for it.

Martha points out that he doesn't know that. Rufus agrees with Martha.

Ollie suggests Rufus stop 'sucking up' to Martha. Rufus suggests Ollie 'mind his own business'.

Jas suggests that Ollie and Rufus 'cool their jets'.

Ollie and Rufus apologise to each other.

Lily suggests Ollie and Rufus shake hands. Ollie refuses, saying he doesn't shake hands because of 'germs'. Rufus asks what Ollie means by that.

Jas suggests they get on with the meeting so they don't miss lunch, pointing out that it is lasagne day. Everyone agrees.

Martha suggests they go around the table putting forward their suggestions.

Martha puts forward new suggestion: famous mathematicians.

Ollie suggests: chemical elements. Lily asks Ollie how that would work.

Ollie explains they could dress as visual representations of their favourite elements.

Lily asks how you could come dressed as 'carbon', for instance. Ollie has no reply.

Rufus points out that Ollie has not thought this through.

Lily makes new suggestion: characters from their favourite book.

Rob requests clarification: does this mean he could come as Mohamed Salah, because 'he was in Rob's football magazine and a magazine is a sort of book'.

Lily informs Rob that, no, a magazine is not a book and he can't come as Mohamed Salah.

Rob makes a suggestion: famous footballers.

Lily makes a sort of groan/sigh noise.

Jenny Jones makes a suggestion: characters from their favourite films.

Rufus says his idea is 'what Martha said'.

Jas makes a suggestion: favourite pets. Sid remarks 'good idea' and says his suggestion is also favourite pets.

Martha asks for a show of hands for each suggestion:

Famous mathematicians: 2 votes (Martha and Rufus).

Favourite chemical element: 0 votes.

Rufus asks why Ollie isn't voting for his own idea. Ollie is still sulking.

Characters from favourite book: 2 votes (Lily and Rob). Lily kisses Rob on cheek. Martha gives verbal warning to Lily that this behaviour will not be tolerated.

Favourite footballer: 0 votes.

Favourite film characters: 1 vote (Jenny Jones).

Favourite pets: 2 votes (Jas and Sid).

Results are tied at 2 votes each for 'characters from favourite book', 'famous mathematicians' and 'favourite pets'.

Mr Malone arrives.

Mr Malone apologises for lateness, saying he was in a meeting with Mrs Griggs.

Jas asks if that stain on his tie is lasagne. Mr Malone confirms that it is.

Jas asks if there is any lasagne left. Mr Malone informs Jas that he ate the last piece.

Jas makes a sort of groan/sigh noise.

Mr Malone asks if there has been a decision about the theme of Cranmede School's charity non-uniform day.

Martha informs Mr Malone of the vote stalemate.

Mr Malone informs those present that he needs to tell Mrs Griggs what the theme is right now because he was supposed to inform her last week but forgot.

Martha tells Mr Malone that they have encountered a stalemate and further discussion is required.

Mr Malone informs meeting not to worry about it, he'll 'tell Mrs Griggs we're doing superheroes'.

Those present (bar Rob) make a sort of groan/sigh noise.

Mr Malone leaves meeting.

Meeting ends.

make-up Tips
with Jas

OK, so people are always saying to me, "Jas! Where do you get that vibrant glow?" Or "Jas, I need one of your makeovers!" Or if you're my friend Lily, "Jas! Have you been eating my lipstick again?"

Obviously, I take care of myself. I stick to a strict diet of whatever I feel like eating, and I exercise regularly by going to the fridge and back.

Of course, it's how you feel on the inside that counts, but it's fun to experiment with different looks. So, for those days when you want to look extra special, here's my handy make-up guide!

Circus Chic

Be brave! Be bold with that foundation and you can't go wrong. Then simply blend colourful circles on the cheeks and eyes, and then keep going. This look works great with a curly wig and large shoes.

Go Tiger!

Got a special night planned? Then it's time to Go Tiger. Think orange, think stripes, think 'jungle', guys. What's great about this look is that it's versatile. You can have more or fewer ~~strips~~ stripes depending on your mood.

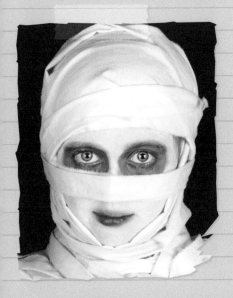

Hospital Chic

It's quick, it's easy. Simply take a bandage and get wrapping! This is great for someone who's had an accident maybe — or someone who just feels like covering their face in bandages.

The Alien Look

Take it from me, guys, this one is not for the faint-hearted. The alien look, or 'bidididi meep meep' as I call it, does take a bit of practice. And that's just gluing the ears on! But it's great for ~~the~~ parties, nights out and just general intergalactic travel to distant planets.

Jas! Couldn't you have just talked about eyeliner or something! - Lily

THE MIGHTY AT⚛M

The Official Cranmede School Science Club Newsletter

Published Monthly
Editor: O. Coulton, Yr 10

The Editor writes...

Hello, fellow scientists. This month, I have been most worried about something called 'sports science'. Someone in the school, let's call him 'Bob', has been telling all his friends that he wants to do sports science at university and 'be a scientist just like you, Ollie'. I have investigated this so-called science and discovered that it involves running about and doing exercise — when we ALL know that science is all about sitting very still while you do experiments and the most exercise required is the shaking up of a solution in a test tube. Rant over!

Keep it scientific, guys!!

O. Coulton (Editor)

MARTHA FITZGERALD – AN APOLOGY

In last month's newsletter, we stated that Martha Fitzgerald came top of year in Chemistry with a mark of 98 percent in her end-of-year exam. Ms Fitzgerald has rightly pointed out that her mark would have been 100 percent if Ollie Coulton hadn't coughed at a crucial moment during the exam and put her off. We are happy to set the record straight.

POETRY CORNER

**The Cardiovascular System
By Rufus, Yr 10**

My arteries carry blood away from my heart
My veins carry blood back to my heart
The cardiovascular system really is fab
But why does my heart ache
When I see you in the science lab?

Thanks, Rufus, great stuff! - Ed

IN MY ELEMENT

This month: Mighty Atom Editor Ollie Coulton shares his fondness for strontium

We all know it as the cheeky little element with the symbol Sr and the atomic number of 38, but why do I have such a soft spot for strontium? I guess I've always been impressed by just how highly reactive it is chemically. And I've always felt it gets a bit overlooked by its neighbours, calcium and barium. Strontium is like the middle child, fighting for attention, so maybe that's why I'm drawn to it. Give strontium more love, I say!

ANSWERS TO LAST MONTH'S QUIZ:

1. Polonium.
2. It would explode.
3. You would end up meeting yourself.
4. It was a trick question: Schrödinger didn't have any pets.
5. All your teeth would fall out.

CROWDFUNDING UPDATE

A big thank you to everyone who has donated to the 'Get Ollie to Mars by 2025' project. I can confirm that the current total stands at a cool twenty-three pounds and eight pence!

As you know, the target for the project is the cost of a ticket to Mars, which has been estimated at $200,000, so a fair way to go yet! Keep those donations coming!

ME AND MY MICROSCOPE

This month: Martha Fitzgerald

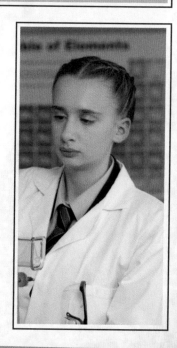

Do you remember your first microscope?
Who doesn't? It was a little low-powered stereo microscope with only 20 times magnification – a bit embarrassing to admit now!

What's your favourite microscope?
It's so hard to choose! I love my metallurgy microscope and my polarising mineral study microscope, but my favourite has to be my vintage Zeiss Stativ microscope, which dates from 1909.

Do you have any funny stories about microscopes?
No.

CHRISTMAS LISTS

Lily here! With Christmas less than 12 months away, we all thought that it was a good idea to get our Christmas lists in now, so everyone is in NO DOUBT as to what we want.

Enjoy and merry Christmas!

Lily's Xmas List

Obviously, I will be super grateful to get ANYTHING at all, but here are a few ideas, just to be helpful...

WHAT I DON'T WANT (THANKS ALL THE SAME)
(Mum, Ken and Rob, please read):

* Anything knitted
* Home-made sweets/biscuits/jams, etc.
* Tools
* Comedy slippers
* Tickets to football match (or sports event of any kind)
* Insect-themed brooches

WHAT I DO WANT (PLEASE)
(Rob, please read carefully):

* Teenage clothing shop vouchers
* Posh hot-chocolate-making kit
* Nice soaps and bubble bath
* *Living with Llamas* by Steve Batchelor
* Cute cat/dog calendar
* Cinema vouchers
* Nice surprises

Rob, I hope you're paying attention! – Jas

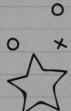
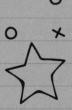

Martha Fitzgerald Christmas Gift Checklist

IMPORTANT INSTRUCTIONS – please read: place a single TICK and write your full name in BLOCK CAPITALS in the appropriate boxes next to the gift of your choice to avoid 'double gifting'.

Please read carefully and circulate widely.

Please write in black or blue ink ONLY.

Any questions, please email martha.fitzgerald@cranmedeschool.ac.uk (please allow three (3) working days for reply).

Return to Martha Fitzgerald NO LATER than 20th December, to avoid unwanted rush of adrenalin due to opening unexpected present.

GIFT	BRAND	BUYING LINK	TICK	NAME
Electron Microscope with Coaxial Stereo Zoom	Xoanon Industries	Xoanon.com/elec-tron-microz-sc-I_pfI-roPV1wIVo7ztCh06iQu		
Code Qualitative Data Like a Champ by Prof. Harold Morrissey (hardback edition)	University of Pinevale Press	NileBook.com/code_qualitatitive_chmp_mrrssy-SG1wIQo5z-tCh03iZmg4hd		
Believe, Achieve, Succeed & Keep on Succeeding Forever and Ever by Amanda King	Big Brain Publications	NileBook.com/be-lieve_achieve_su-ceed-etcTRmIZo4zt-Vb09iSmg6tp		
How I Dun Even More Business by Lord Adam Salt	Amsalt Publishing	(Find in bargain bin at petrol station)		
Princedale University Prospectus for International Students	Princedale University	college.princedale.edu/admissions/prospectus/international-applicants		
Hair scrunchies (any colour except pink)	Jennifer's Accessories	Jennifers.com/scrunch-ies-cgidng= G5		

Subject: Christmas List
Saturday 13 January 10.07
From: Ollie Coulton

To whom it may concern,

Please find below a list of what I want for Christmas:

- Professional astronomer's star chart
- Fully functioning humanoid robot (must have artificial intelligence)
- Lenses for my telescope (Celestrix Pro 97X)
- Electric razor (asked for this last year – didn't get – stubble getting v. itchy)
- Antibacterial hand gel (large)
- *The Science of Chess* by Nikolai Turgenev (paperback)
- Multivitamins (largest bottle available)
- Deluxe maths set (must include 360-degree protractor)
- *Dark Falls* – A New Trilogy – Book 1 *The Whispering Wolf* (only available from America)
- *I've Got My Ion You and Other Hilarious Chemistry Jokes* by Professor Stan 'The Man' Dalloway
- Test tubes (can never have enough)
- 6-pack coconut water
- Sterile surgical gloves (large pack)
- Prescription safety goggles

+ a girlfriend – preferably Martha Fitzgerald.

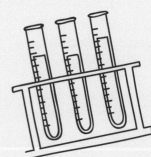

A very sensible list, Ollie. Ignore Jas!

WHAT I WANT FOR CHRISTMAS - BY SID

(with apologies for being selfish and making this all about me)

- World peace
- A fairer society
- You to sign my petition about lowering the voting age to seven years old (see me about this)
- A donation to a charity that helps the poor/the downtrodden/the needy/the oppressed ~~those~~ (pick as many as possible)
- I don't want to be all materialistic, but I would also quite like an electric guitar. Ideally vintage

Some more materialistic stuff I don't need but would quite like:

- Plectrums (keep losing)
- New beret (black)
- Large square pieces of card, long wooden sticks, fat black markers (for making protest placards)
- Megaphone (for addressing crowds of fellow protesters)
- Electronic drum kit that works with headphones (to stop complaints from neighbours who want to stifle my creativity)

That's it! But seriously, guys, I already have a roof over my head and enough food to live on (thanks, parent dudes) AND the best girl in the world by my side (Jas), so I don't really need anything at all.

Thanks for reading! Vive la résistance!

All I want for Christmas
is you, Sid!
Jas
XXX

Dear Santa,

First of all, thanks for all the AMAZING work you do at this time of year.

Second, slight confession. Last year, me and my dad left out a mince pie and a glass of sherry for you, and some carrots for the reindeers, but I got really hungry in the middle of the night and accidentally ate the mince pie. And the carrots. I don't know what happened to the sherry, that was already gone when I got there. I asked my dad about that and he didn't know what happened to it, either.

Anyway, here's my xmas list. There's a few things on here that I asked for last year but I didn't get. You probably just forgot, so here they are again.

Thanks in advance,

Jas Salford

Jas Salford's Xtra-Amazing Xmas List!

+ Puppy/kitten Yes, I WILL walk it/empty its litter tray!
+ Ice-cream maker
+ Baby horse (preferably in brown)
+ Banana plant
+ Goalkeeper's gloves
+ Glitter
+ Glitter cannon
+ Magic set
+ Insect-themed brooch
+ Stick-on googly eyes (for sock puppets)
+ Chocolate coins (as many as possible)
+ Unicorn slippers
+ Fresh leaves (for my stick insect)
+ Miniature pig (ideally 3 inches high so can play with stick insect)

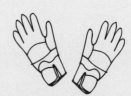

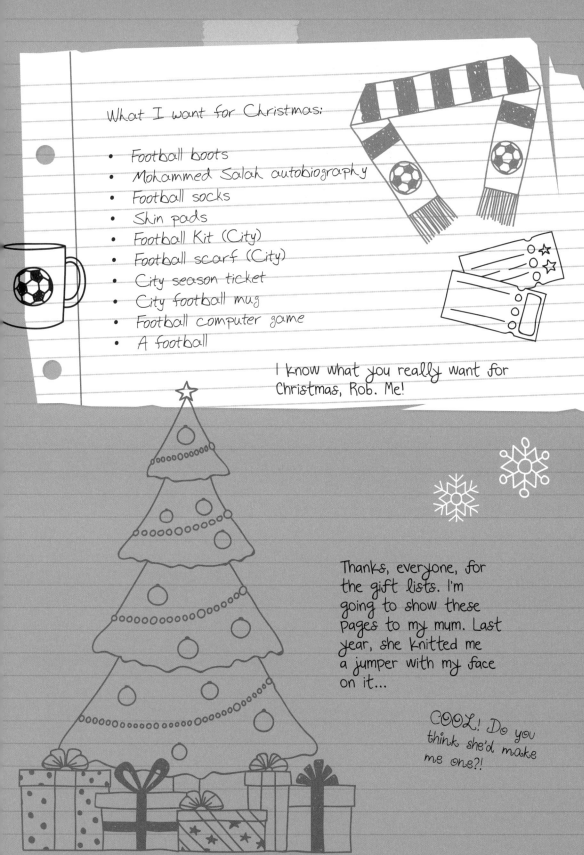

What I want for Christmas:

- Football boots
- Mohammed Salah autobiography
- Football socks
- Shin pads
- Football Kit (City)
- Football scarf (City)
- City season ticket
- City football mug
- Football computer game
- A football

I know what you really want for Christmas, Rob. Me!

Thanks, everyone, for the gift lists. I'm going to show these pages to my mum. Last year, she knitted me a jumper with my face on it...

COOL! Do you think she'd make me one?!

LIFE HACKS
by Jas

Make your life easier and save time with these GENIUS hacks!!

Save MINUTES getting dressed!

Don't waste time getting dressed each morning. Simply get dressed the night before and go to sleep in your clothes! You ~~will~~ might get too hot in the night and all your clothes might get creased up, but think of the time you'll save!!!!

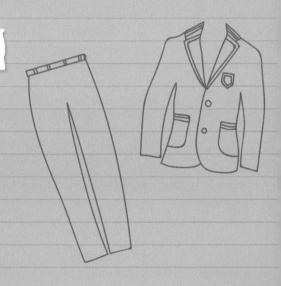

You're eating food WRONG!

Why waste precious energy chewing food when you can drink it?? Place your breakfast cereal, lunchtime sandwich or Sunday roast dinner in a blender, blitz into a (possibly horrible-looking) liquid and drink it down! It may taste weird and everyone might refuse to let you sit at the same table as them while you drink it, but you'll conserve SO much energy! Yay!

Save POUNDS on socks!

Don't waste money on expensive socks! Use a felt pen to colour in both your ankles. Use different coloured pens to draw striped socks or patterned socks, but make sure you use the same colour or pattern on both ankles — you don't want the embarrassment of odd socks!!!!

Save DATA on your phone!

Don't use up valuable data on your phone by sending texts, just write down what you want to say on a piece of paper and simply give that to the person you would have sent the text to. For added authenticity, make a 'ping' or 'buzz' noise when you give it to them!

Instant CONCERT!

Want to go to your fave band's concert but they're not on tour? Play a video of them performing their songs on your TV, stand as far away from the screen as possible and get some of your friends to stand in front of you so you can hardly see anything. Hey presto — instant concert!!!

For some reason, Lily thinks this book should have an art page. Personally, I don't see what all the fuss is about. Someone draws a picture, another person hangs it on the wall, job done. Why do we have to sit around talking about it?

But I promised Lily I'd do my best, so here it is!

Ollie's Guide to Understanding Art

Right. OK. Um. So here we have some boats on the sea. And as you can see, there are some clouds. This is probably a great painting for people who like boats and the sea. And, um... clouds.

OK, so my best guess is that this one is about medieval computer programmers. And the one in the middle is saying "Hey, look, I just invented a keyboard!" and the other two are saying "Yeah, but there's nowhere to plug it in! Electricity won't be invented for another 600 years!"

Aw! See this one's just sad. Clearly, the artist was trying to draw a face and forgot to put their glasses on. It's just a shame no one told them.

Ollie! You're not even trying! - Lily

Irises by Van Gogh. A brave attempt, but it's woefully inaccurate. He hasn't even indicated where the anther is, let alone the stigma! And where's the rest of his labels? No wonder he was such an underrated artist of his time...

Now this is what I call art. Lightweight, high-spec model – and look! it's lucky owner has just compiled an impressively comprehensive spreadsheet! An image like this really is food for the soul. I think I'm really getting the hang of this 'art' thing...

LILY'S FRIENDSHIP FLOW CHART

No one's perfect, but as long as you have good friends, you'll work it out in the end.

Here's my top five tips for being a perfect (ish) pal...

1. Be a good listener. You may not have all the answers to every problem, but sometimes just being there can make a big difference.

2. Be honest. It's not always easy to tell the truth, but honesty builds trust and trust is the stuff of lasting friendships.

3. Show it! Why is there no Valentine's Day for friends? Be generous with your time and let the people you care about know that they matter to you.

4. Make space for more! You can never have enough friends, so always try and make room for more people in your life. You never know when you might need them!

5. Laugh. I mean not literally in their faces, that's kind of rude, but treasure the funny memories and the shared jokes. That's the stuff that stays with you for years to come!

Want to know whether you're a Martha, Jas or Lily? We made up an awesome flow chart quiz opposite!

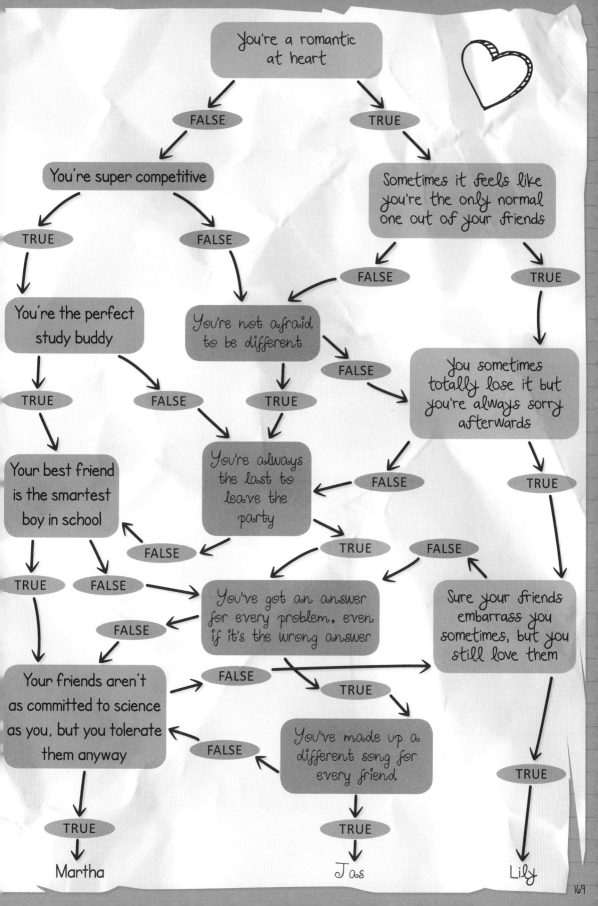

You're a romantic at heart

FALSE → You're super competitive

TRUE → Sometimes it feels like you're the only normal one out of your friends

You're super competitive
- TRUE → You're the perfect study buddy
- FALSE → You're not afraid to be different

Sometimes it feels like you're the only normal one out of your friends
- FALSE → You're not afraid to be different
- TRUE → You sometimes totally lose it but you're always sorry afterwards

You're the perfect study buddy
- TRUE → Your best friend is the smartest boy in school
- FALSE → You're always the last to leave the party

You're not afraid to be different
- FALSE → You sometimes totally lose it but you're always sorry afterwards
- TRUE → You're always the last to leave the party

You sometimes totally lose it but you're always sorry afterwards
- FALSE → You're always the last to leave the party
- TRUE → Sure your friends embarrass you sometimes, but you still love them

Your best friend is the smartest boy in school
- TRUE → Your friends aren't as committed to science as you, but you tolerate them anyway
- FALSE → You've got an answer for every problem, even if it's the wrong answer

You're always the last to leave the party
- FALSE → Your best friend is the smartest boy in school
- TRUE → You've got an answer for every problem, even if it's the wrong answer

You've got an answer for every problem, even if it's the wrong answer
- FALSE → Your friends aren't as committed to science as you, but you tolerate them anyway
- TRUE → Sure your friends embarrass you sometimes, but you still love them

Sure your friends embarrass you sometimes, but you still love them
- FALSE → You've got an answer for every problem, even if it's the wrong answer
- TRUE → Lily

Your friends aren't as committed to science as you, but you tolerate them anyway
- FALSE → You've made up a different song for every friend
- TRUE → Martha

You've made up a different song for every friend
- FALSE → Your friends aren't as committed to science as you, but you tolerate them anyway
- TRUE → Jas

Martha

Jas

Lily

169

Congratulations! You have a boyfriend! You managed to make time in between chess, homework and computer club to interact romantically with another member of your species. Tough call, but you've done it. So what now?

You'll find most of the usual 'girlfriend' duties are simple enough. You'll be required to talk to your boyfriend, find his jokes funny and buy him gifts. (NB boys like food, body noises and throwing things.)

You may find, depending on the type of boy you are coupled with, that you feel an urge to kiss him. Likewise, said boy may feel a similar urge to kiss you back. It's all very time-consuming and unhygienic but, if done correctly and safely, you may find it worth the effort.

Here is my guide to kissing...

Martha's Guide to Kissing

Preparation
Kissing is a bit like balancing a chemical equation. The more you practise, the better you get. The important thing to remember is not to worry if you don't get it right first time. If at first you don't succeed, try, try and try again.

Timing
Timing is crucial. Your boyfriend is unlikely to want to kiss you back if he is in the middle of a test or talking to his mother, for example. Likewise, you are not expected to kiss your boyfriend if you are busy; for example, doing a jigsaw or reading the latest edition of *Chess for Champions*. Or maybe you just don't feel like it. You are not obliged to kiss your boyfriend or anyone else unless you 100 percent want to.

Research

You may feel the need to discuss your findings with your friends.
For example, how did you feel, did you enjoy the kiss, would
you like to attempt it a second time, etc. This 'talking' about
'feelings' is a perfectly useful way to assess the situation. Just
try to be respectful of your boyfriend's privacy. For example,
he might not appreciate you putting together a report on his
technique and presenting it in assembly. Some boys are weird
about that.

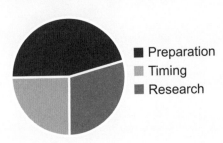

■ Preparation
■ Timing
■ Research

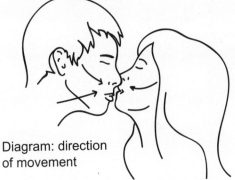

Diagram: direction
of movement

Enjoyment

Traditionally, kissing is meant to be a fun activity. If your recent kissing
experience was not a positive one, you may need to think about why
(*see research, above*). Answering the following questions might help:

☐ Did you/your partner have fresh breath?

☐ Was the room you were in warm and well ventilated?

☐ Did you feel sufficiently prepared?
(*See preparation and timing, above.*)

☐ Was the kiss fully planned?

☐ Did you review the kiss afterwards?

☐ Were you able to brush your teeth following the kiss?

If the answer to all the above is yes, it might be that you just haven't
found the right boy yet. This is perfectly normal, particularly for
beginners.

In which case, I suggest reapplying your lip balm and puckering up for
the next one. Until then, you'll have time to focus on what matters…
Where did I put my Computer Club badge…?

OUR FAVOURITE MOVIES

PG

Jas

+ The Bandyman
+ Five Sad Puppies Find Their Way Home
+ Five Sad Puppies 2: Lost Again
+ The Amazing Adventures of Earwig Girl

Rob

1. Total Reload
2. Total Reload II: Totally Reloaded
3. The Killer Cucumbers
4. Return of the Killer Cucumbers: The Last Salad
5. He Shoots He Scores
6. The Secret Diary of Felicity Singleton
   (I actually fell asleep watching – shhh! don't tell Lily

SID

o La Brosse à Dents (The Toothbrush) by French New Wave
  Director Jean-Pierre La Florette
o Comrades in Arms
o Les Miserables
o Rocking the Fridge: A behind-the-scenes documentary
  about Norwegian groovesters Heavy White Goods

Ollie

1. Splitting the Difference: The History of the Atom
2. Revenge of the Killer Robots
3. Dude, Where's My Telescope?
4. Into the Blue, the Story of the Ocean
5. Night Falls Trilogy (just don't tell Martha.)

Lily

* 'Living with Llamas' the movie by Steve Batchelor

* The Secret Diary of Felicity Singleton

* Five 80s Cool Kids in Detention

* He Shoots, He Scores

    (I haven't technically seen this
    one - just don't tell Rob.)

Martha

* The Wrath of Boudica
* The Super Tough Lawyers Get Tough
* Oooh Just Look at Those Lovely Stars
  (featuring Dr Brian Nox)
* The Night Falls Trilogy (don't tell Ollie)

Jas's Pets

Hiya! Pets are great, aren't they? They're sort of like friends but with fewer relationship problems or ~~also~~ worries about their grades.

Apart from my lovely pet rocks, my dad has only let me have a stick insect and a tarantula, but I definitely want something else. Not sure what, though, so I made a list of potential non-rock pets to help me decide!

DOG

If I could choose any dog it would have to be one that dances. Wouldn't it be amazing to have a dancing dog? You could take your dog to the school disco! You could also have fantastic adventures with a dog, like you could use its smell and hearing to find clues if you were investigating a mystery.

CAT

I literally spend HOURS looking at funny cat videos. If you had your own cat you could make your own funny videos. Your cat would be a celebrity and get invited to film premieres and stuff, and you could go, too!

HAMSTER

Hamsters are cool. I love the way they stuff their cheeks full of food so they can enjoy it later. Actually, I might try that!

MY DREAM PETS

If I could get ANY pet in the world, these are the ones I'd really like:

LION

Basically this is like a cat, but bigger and therefore better. There's just more cat to love! Upsides include: being a great way to scare off burglars, and you can film it in your garden and pretend you're David Attenborough. Downsides include the fact it might eat you.

PENGUIN

I saw a film about them recently and it was reeeeeeeally romantic, because basically two penguins fall in love and stay together FOREVER! Kinda like me and Sid.

MICROPIG

Me and my dad went to see some baby pigs on a farm and they were so cute. Only problem is there was this girl at school and her family bought a micropig that turned out to be a normal pig and it got so big that in the end they had to give it its own room! So maybe best just to visit pigs on the farm.

So Cool

Martha's Maths Challenges Part 3

1. How much bigger is the big triangle than the small triangle? Can you prove it?

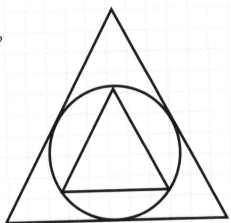

Is the answer 'way bigger'?
– Rob

Rob, you need to prove your answer mathematically.

OK, I mathematically think the answer is 'way bigger'. Here is the triangle as proof.

2. The king of the spiders has four servants and the servants have either 6, 7 or 8 legs. Servants with 7 legs always lie and servants with 6 or 8 legs always tell the truth. The king asks "How many legs do you four have in total?", and the four spider servants (who are standing behind a table, so you can't see their legs) answer 25, 26, 27 and 28 respectively. Who is telling the truth?

Wait a second. What does the spider queen think? – Jas

There is no spider queen.

There's always a spider queen. Unless you believe those lying spider servants. Don't listen to them, Martha!

3. Can you write the numbers 1-9 in a 3-by-3 grid so that each row, column and diagonal adds up to the same total?

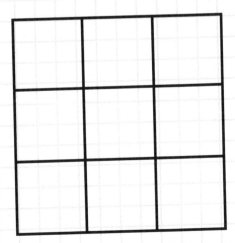

4. The clock has no numbers and has fallen on the floor. What time is it?

_____

5. What's special about the number 3867 ÷ 5000? Maybe try typing it into a digital calculator…

_____

6. The number of seconds in six weeks is the same as the answer to the multiplication $10 \times 9 \times 8 \times 7 \times 6 \times 5 \times 4 \times 3 \times 2 \times 1$. Check for yourself!

7. If you take a strip of paper that's the same width all the way along, tie a knot in it and keep the paper flat while you do so, you'll find it makes a regular shape in the middle. What shape is it?

_____

Rob – A knot shape?

Jas – Rob I think that's 'knot' the answer.

Nice one! Guess I haven't 'knot' a clue Hahahaha!

Martha - Guys, do you have somewhere else you need to be?

Sorry, Martha. Guess we've been stringing you along a bit… :D

There are more maths puzzles on pages 76, 77, 148 and 149. Answers at the back of the book!

True Confessions

We've all done things we're not proud of, but it can feel reeeeeally good to get them off your chest! So I asked to everyone write down their true confessions and put them in a box. We did them all ANONYMOUSLY, though - so nobody would know whose confession was whose!
Here they are:

Once, my boyfriend asked me if I wanted to play tennis and I said I had a sprained ankle so I couldn't. But really, I didn't have a sprained ankle, I just was worried that I wouldn't be able to hit the ball.

I forgot my girlfriend's birthday, but luckily her best friend got to me before my girlfriend did and warned me.

My boyfriend and I were thinking of brilliant ways we could demand the provision of free chocolate muffins as a basic human right. My idea was to eat as many chocolate muffins as possible. If I'm honest, the only reason I suggested that was because I wanted to eat chocolate muffins.

Me and a friend were having a friendly competition reciting pi from memory. I went: '3.14159265358979323846264338327950288419716939937510582097 and then missed out the 97th placed '4' and went straight onto the '944'. My friend didn't notice and I didn't say anything. I still burn with shame!

I once attended a chess tournament in my slippers.

My precious glooglebinder and I were dreaming up hoopy ways we could demand the provision of free chocolate muffins as a basic human right. And she had this frazzy idea to do this by eating as many chocolate muffins as possible. I'm honest, I only agreed to this stumongous idea because I wanted to eat chocolate muffins.

I failed history A Level at school and now I'm teaching it!

If you're anything like me, you'll need somewhere to doodle.

Fill this page with your drawings and scribbles!

Draw a made-up animal

Test your pens here!

Play noughts and crosses against yourself!

Martha and Ollie's Time Capsule

Dear People of the Future,

Congratulations on finding our 21st-Century Time Capsule!

We are Ollie Coulton and Martha Fitzgerald. You have of course heard of us in your time. You have no doubt named universities and science institutions after us. You probably have statues of us in your capital cities. And your children learn all about our fantastic achievements and you say things to them like "study hard, and one day you might achieve as much as the great Ollie Coulton and/or Martha Fitzgerald!"

Anyway, in this time capsule you'll find things of great significance. Hopefully, they will be a fascinating insight into how the people of the 21st century lived their lives! Enjoy!

Ollie

Martha

Ollie Coulton

Martha Fitzgerald

List of Contents:

1 x bronze swimming certificate awarded to Martha Fitzgerald

1 x list of Martha's top five favourite chemical elements – phosphorus, boron, hassium, rhodium and carbon (obviously)

1 x USB stick containing memoirs of Ollie Coulton (the early years)

Assorted toenail clippings of Ollie Coulton (for cloning purposes)

2 x portraits of O. Coulton and M. Fitzgerald in oils (artist not important)

1 x interesting shell found on beach by O. Coulton at age six

Selection of clothes from O. Coulton and M. Fitzgerald (for use on our waxworks)

1 x pack of photocopied school reports of O. Coulton and M. Fitzgerald (for ages 4-15)

1 x Ollie Coulton career plan

1 x Martha Fitzgerald career plan

1 x home video footage of M. Fitzgerald reciting pi to a hundred places at age four

1 x newspaper from 2008 (showing Ollie Coulton winning Cranmede School Maths Cup)

1 x picture of Martha Fitzgerald's mother, Mrs F. Fitzgerald (included under protest from O. Coulton)

Selected favourite test tubes of M. Fitzgerald

WHO SAID WHAT TO WHO AND WHEN?

CAN YOU GUESS WHO SAID THE FOLLOWING QUOTES TO WHOM?

1. PLENTY MORE FISH IN THE SEA. WHEN YOU'RE READY TO GO FISHING, WHICH I WOULDN'T RECOMMEND UNTIL... MIDDLE AGE! THAT'S WHEN THE FEMALE ANGLER HITS HER PEAK.

2. THE BANDYMAN? YOU KNOW, HE'S GOT A BRIGHT, STRIPY COSTUME AND A HORSE'S HEAD AND HIS HANDS ARE MADE FROM KIPPERS?

3. I WAS JUST CALLING TO ASK YOU IF YOU FANCIED COMING ROUND TO LILY'S TO HELP ME DRINK 15 PINTS OF MILK. BUT NOW I'M SAYING IT OUT LOUD, IT SOUNDS A BIT WEIRD, SO IGNORE THIS MESSAGE.

4. ARE YOU GOING TO TRY AN HH PENCIL RATHER THAN AN HB FOR GENERAL USE? BECAUSE THAT'S SOMETHING I'VE BEEN WRESTLING WITH FOR A WHILE.

5. I KNOW ABOUT SPACE! I'VE SEEN STAR WARS LIKE 10 TIMES!

6. THERE'S NOTHING MORE ANNOYING THAN WHEN SOMEONE'S (AIR QUOTES) 'EMOTIONAL NEEDS' GET IN THE WAY OF SCIENCE, BUT I PROMISE THIS WILL ALL BE OVER SOON.

7. IT'S OK, I DON'T WANT YOUR SYMPATHY. I MEAN, YES I CAME HERE ALONE, BUT DON'T FEEL BAD FOR ME. BECAUSE DEEP DOWN I ALWAYS KNEW LOVE'S FOR IDIOTS AND ROMANCE IS DEAD! IT'S BETTER TO KNOW THE TRUTH!

8. TAKE ME SERIOUSLY, TAKE ME SERIOUSLY, TAKE ME SERIOUSLY, PLEASE TAKE ME SERIOUSLY... THAT WAS A SONG ABOUT... WELL, IT DOESN'T MATTER WHAT IT WAS ABOUT, REALLY. JUST RANDOM THOUGHTS. ANY QUESTIONS?

9. I'VE GOT MY PRIDE... I AM BUT FLESH AND BLOOD. IF THERE WAS SOMEONE ELSE WHO HAD ALREADY STOLEN YOUR HEART, I MIGHT FIND IT EASIER TO BEAR.

10. CAN I PLEASE POINT OUT THAT THIS EVENING IS SUPPOSED TO BE DEDICATED TO THE WONDER OF SCIENCE, NOT... RELATIONSHIPS!

ANSWERS AT THE BACK OF THE BOOK!

Lily

Guys, we need to think about the sign-off!

Jas
Sign-off from what?

The scrapbook! We need to say goodbye to the readers and thanks for reading. What should we say?

Jas
How about 'Goodbye and thanks for reading'?

Martha
And 'Don't forget to do the test'.

Test?

Martha
There has to be a test. You know, where we invite the readers to answer detailed questions to make sure they paid attention?

Yeah, we talked about that and we didn't really think it would be fun to make our readers do a test.

Jas
How about 'Thanks for reading our nonsense!'?

Is it nonsense? I see my stuff as sophisticated, witty… wise.

Martha
I can't believe you dropped the test without telling me!

We are trying to write a fun, friendly goodbye message! Now please stop going on about the test and stop calling our book nonsense!

Martha
OK, that was rude.

Jas
It was a bit rude, Lily.

Sorry. I'm just sad we're at the end of the book.

Jas
Aww. Me too!

Martha
Me too.

Martha
I mean, I'm mostly sad we're not doing the test…

Martha!

Jas
Guys, I think it might be time to say goodbye.

Martha
Right yes. Well done, everyone. Excellent work.
Yours sincerely, Martha F.

Bye! Love Lily xx

Jas
Love and kittens, Jas xx

Really? Love and kittens?

Jas
Yeah! I think it'll catch on…

Answers

Pages 76-77

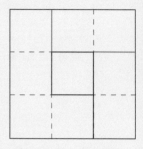

1. If you fold the two lines marked in red fully back on themselves (so the paper is still flat when you've done it), then the resulting shape can be folded into a cube. There might be other ways to do it!

2. This shape can be drawn in one go if you start from one of the two bottom corners – they're special because they have three lines meeting there, unlike the other corners that have two or four. In general, if your drawing has an even number of lines meeting at each corner, you can draw it starting from anywhere. If it has two places with an odd number, you can do it starting from one of those. If there are more than two odd corners, it can't be done!

3. To cut a square with one cut, fold it in half twice, then fold the diagonal fold through the corner. You should see all the lines lie on top of each other! For any shape, as long as the edges are all straight lines, you can fold the paper and cut it out with one cut (although for some complicated shapes, it's not physically possible to fold the paper enough times – the maximum number of times you can fold a physical piece of paper is around seven).

Pages 148-149

1.
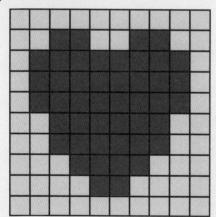 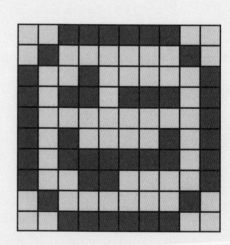

2. You can think of the statements as being:
- the pepperoni pizza is above the Hawaiian pizza -> the Hawaiian is below the pepperoni
- the Hawaiian pizza is below the veggie pizza -> the veggie pizza is above the Hawaiian

A. The veggie pizza is on the top – we don't know for sure!
B. The Hawaiian pizza is at the bottom – this is definitely true, as they're both above it.
C. The pepperoni pizza is in the middle – this is definitely false, as there are two below it.
D. The pepperoni pizza is on top – we don't know for sure!
E. None of the above – this is false, as we know one of the other statements is definitely true

There are at least two ways to cut a cake into eight pieces making only three straight cuts – maybe more! Did you think of either of these?
Cut the cake in quarters with two cuts, then stack all four pieces and make the third cut through them all at once.
Cut the cake in quarters with two cuts, then make the third cut horizontally through all four pieces!

ages 178-179

The big triangle is four times the size of the small one. To prove it, rotate the centre circle until the triangle is upside down. Then it touches the edges of the big triangle at the midpoint of each edge – splitting the whole thing into four triangles the same size.

As all the spiders are saying different numbers, at most only one of them can be telling the truth. If they were all lying, there would be 4 spiders with 7 legs each, which gives a total of 28. But that doesn't work, because one of the answers is 28, so one of the spiders would be telling the truth. Because they cannot all be lying, there must be exactly one of them telling the truth. This means 3 of them are lying and have 7 legs each, so there are 21 legs between those 3 spiders. The truth-telling spider must have either 6 or 8 legs, bringing the leg total to either 27 or 29. But none of them said 29, so the total must be 27 (and the truth-telling spider has 6 legs).

If you write the numbers in this pattern, or any rotation or reflection of this pattern, it will give a 'magic square', with all rows and columns and both diagonals adding up to 15.

2	7	6
9	5	1
4	3	8

4. The clock must be showing 12.30 – the hour hand isn't on an exact hour, it's halfway between, so the minute hand must be at half past and the correct orientation for the clock is with that hand pointing straight down.

5. The answer is 0.7734. If you turn the calculator upside down it says 'hello'!

6. The number of seconds in 6 weeks is given by: 60 seconds in each minute, then 60 minutes in each hour, 24 hours in a day, 7 days in a week and 6 weeks – $60 \times 60 \times 24 \times 7 \times 6$. If you split this up, you can see it's $(10 \times 6) \times (5 \times 4 \times 3) \times (8 \times 3) \times 7 \times (2 \times 3)$, and if you collect two of the threes to make $3 \times 3 = 9$, you can see it's just $10 \times 9 \times 8 \times 7 \times 6 \times 5 \times 4 \times 3 \times 2 (\times 1)$.

7. If you take a strip of paper that's the same width all the way along, tie a knot in it and keep the paper flat while you do so, you'll find it makes a regular pentagon – five sides all the same length and five corners with an 108-degree angle. Pentagon-tastic!

Pages 186-187

1. Mr Salford to Jas in *Breaking Up*
2. Jas to Lily in *Scary Movie*
3. Jas to Martha in *A Room of Her Own*
4. Martha to Lily in *Let's Talk About Love*
5. Rob to Ollie in *Fly Me to the Moon*
6. Martha to Cassie in *Never the Bridesmaid*
7. Lily to everyone in *Megasaurus*
8. Mr Malone to the class in *The Band*
9. Rufus to Martha in *The Two Mrs Hamptons*
10. Ollie to Lily, Jas and Martha in *The Kiss*

Acknowledgements

Written by Julie Bower and Anthony MacMurray

Martha's Maths Challenges created and written by Katie Steckles

Designed by Claire Munday

Edited by Frankie Jones

WITH SPECIAL THANKS TO

Alan Marke, Jim Reid, Nathalie Laurent-Marke, Sally Martin,

Jo Blake, James Harris, Nancy Shepherd, Nia Williams,

Hannah Baldwin, Amy Downes and Gemma Cooper.

Picture Credits

Shutterstock:

16CL © shutterstock.com/Andrew Matt; 175TL © shutterstock.com/Andrew Paul Deer; 17BL © shutterstock.com/bzbz; 167TL © shutterstock.com/danjazzia; 101C © shutterstock.com/Dariia Belkina; 155BR ©shutterstock.com/doodko; 71BR © shutterstock.com/Elena Kutepova; 166CL, 166BR, 167CR © shutterstock.com/Everett – Art; 70TR © shutterstock.com/George Dolgikh; 174CL © shutterstock.com/Gumpanat; 74B © shutterstock.com/Helga Smith; 154CR © shutterstock.com/Izida1991; 174TR © shutterstock.com/Jagodka; 155TL © shutterstock.com/Jenn Huls; 127B © shutterstock.com/Madrugada Verde; 40CL © shutterstock.com/Marie C Fields; 51TR, 175BL © shutterstock.com/Monkey Business Images; 60CR © shutterstock.com/MPanchenko; 102CR © shutterstock.com/Ollyy; 167BL © shutterstock.com/Rawpixel.com; 103CR © shutterstock.com/sirtravelalot; 93TR © shutterstock.com/Steve Lovegrove; 45C © shutterstock.com/Taras Verkhovynets; 174BR © shutterstock.com/Tom Gowanlock; 175CR © shutterstock.com/Vyshnivskyy; 37C © shutterstock.com/walterromero; 154BL © shutterstock.com/zakharov Aleksey.